THE MIDLIFE KITCHEN

HEALTH-BOOSTING RECIPES FOR MIDLIFE & BEYOND

MIMI SPENCER & SAM RICE

Nutritional Consultant: Dr Sarah Schenker

MITCHELL BEAZLEY

CONTENTS

Are you at a point in your life where health is becoming more of a priority? Are you confused by ever-changing headlines that contrive to make the simple act of eating a peril rather than a pleasure? So were we. *The Midlife Kitchen* is our response.

Welcome to the Midlife Kitchen

We think that midlife is not a time to be concerned with food fads and foibles, but rather a glorious opportunity to wrest back control of your eating in the interests of health, happiness and a long life. Taste must certainly come first, but with health firmly snapping at its heels, underpinned by well-established nutritional common sense. We also appreciate the need for speed: busy lives require simple, sustaining recipes that incorporate health-giving ingredients without too much fanfare or fuss.

This is what *The Midlife Kitchen* is all about: eating gorgeous ingredients in the most delicious combinations to give yourself the best possible odds for a healthy future. The recipes here are intended to be rejuvenating, restorative and reviving, a way of future-proofing your life through your forties, fifties and well beyond.

You won't find restrictions here. We firmly believe in inclusivity; unless you have an allergy or intolerance, incorporating as many diverse ingredients across all the food groups is, we think, essential for maintaining optimum health and wellbeing. There's no cod science either. We focus on foods for which there is an overwhelming body of evidence supporting their nutritional CVs, with each ingredient selected for the midlife benefits it offers.

We hope you find inspiration in these pages to mark a new chapter in your relationship with food, one where you can cook fantastically tasty dishes, safe in the knowledge that they're also doing you the power of good.

OUR STORY

The idea for *The Midlife Kitchen* was born on a holiday in Bali, where Sam now lives. We met years ago, as many of us do, at the school gates, and we've remained firm friends ever since. We always knew we were destined to collaborate on a project, but work, family life and the mad whirl of the world got in the way... until now. Many crazy schemes came and went, but when we came up with the idea for *The Midlife Kitchen* we were convinced it was something we just had to do.

We knew that there were many, many midlifers out there who, just like us, wanted to improve their diet. We'd both cruised through the drinking years and the party decades without much of a thought for nutrition; we ate – like so many of us – as if the future would never come. As we worked through our twenties and thirties, skipping breakfast, eating lunch on the run, relying on white carbs and fast food to get us by, nutrition barely registered, and if it did, it was only because we wanted to lose weight in time for summer. When we had kids (four between us), our energies, particularly in the kitchen, were soon devoted to them. But now, as our children have become more independent, we've found we both have some time to invest in ourselves. It feels like a watershed moment in the game, a time to head for the locker room to regroup and work out strategies for the second half of life.

HITTING THE MIDDLE

Midlife is full of surprises, and not all of them are welcome. As actress Gillian Anderson says, 'We think we're invincible in some way, that age isn't going to touch us, so your response when you see the skin on your hands and your forearms changing is "ooh, aah, what the...?"'

The upside, at least, is that we're all going through it – or we will do, one of these days. Perhaps your hair is greying, or you've noticed you don't metabolize alcohol as you did in your twenties. It could be that you don't sleep as well as you once did, or that your energy levels have dipped as your metabolism slows. For many of us, like it or not, it's our mother or father's face that looks back from the mirror. Our parents may be slowing down too, or leaving us; we may have a friend who's had a cancer scare, or a partner with a raised cholesterol score on a routine blood test. Words like peri-menopause and HRT start to crop up in conversation. Hormonal shifts may well have redistributed body fat to accumulate around the middle. Typically, we put on a kilo or two for every four years in middle age (women gain an average of 4.5kg during menopause). So, small alarm bells ring and something tells us it's time to act.

But act we can. Someone wise once said that at the age of 20, we have the health and appearance we inherited; at 50 and beyond, we have the face and body we created. Indeed, for most leading causes of death, our genes are known to account for only about 20 per cent of risk; the rest is directly under our control. It's worth taking a moment to digest that fact: the foods we choose really do make a difference. 'Nutri-epigenetics' is now a major focus of scientific enquiry, where certain vitamins, minerals and plant chemicals have been found to have powerful potential for reducing the risk of age-related disease. Public Health England recently stated that living healthily in midlife can double a person's chances of staying fit and well aged 70 and older, which is something we really can't afford to ignore.

Fortunately for us, modern midlife isn't the burden it once was. These days, it's more a time of opportunity than loss. The age itself has, organically, gradually, found itself redeemed. We like Sharon Stone's take: 'I have absolutely no objection to growing older,' she says. 'I am a stroke survivor so I am extremely grateful to be ageing – I have nothing but gratitude for the passing years. I am ageing – lucky, lucky me!' Both of us would echo the sentiment. There's something about midlife – its experience, its wry understanding of the world, its new freedoms, the fact that we now know and appreciate these singular bodies of ours – that demands we rejoice, not lament.

Today's midlife crisis is more likely to be expressed in a carbon-fibre road bike than in a bright red Porsche. Many of us are already responding to key health messages that we know, at heart, to be true, because following them makes us feel... better. We're naturally cutting our meat intake, lowering our consumption of processed food and white carbs, eating sustainably and consciously to protect our bodies and environment, and we're ever more interested in new ingredients that bring something fresh and vital to our plates. The Midlife Kitchen simply capitalizes on a process that's already in train, often inspired by global culinary traditions – from Bali, Japan, Peru, India and

Someone wise once said that at the age of 20, we have the health and appearance we inherited; at 50 and beyond, we have the face and body we created

the Mediterranean – which have long acknowledged the potent symbiosis between health and nutrition.

Of course, no foods are proven to be 'anti-ageing'; there's no elixir, no magic wand. We can't turn back the clock, but we can, with small changes and minimal effort, stay healthier for longer. The Midlife Kitchen is concerned with 'healthspan' rather than lifespan – extending the number of fit and 'functional' years ahead. As hormone expert Dr Marion Gluck writes, 'The unavoidable reality is that we all age. The real question is *how* we age.' With that in mind, the Midlife Kitchen is categorically pro-ageing, not anti-ageing. We don't fear growing older. We want to embrace it in the knowledge that we are as healthy as we can be.

As we get to 40 and beyond, though, things change. We've both found that our palates have shifted; whether that's down to changes in our sense of taste, an understanding of the fundamentals of good eating, or simply because our bodies are trying to tell us that they need certain nutrients to function properly, we have found that where once we craved pasta we now prefer an interesting salad; the sweet tooth of youth has diminished as the need for intensely savoury, texture-rich foods has increased.

Indeed, in midlife, our nutritional needs are very different from those of our twenties and thirties: we need greater fortification from foods full of vitamins and minerals, to guard against loss of muscle mass and – of particular concern to women – a decrease in bone density. We need more lean protein too (vital for cellular health), a moderate quantity of 'good' slow-burn carbohydrates and plenty of gut-friendly probiotics – while women can benefit from eating foods high in phytoestrogens such as flaxseeds (the holy grain for midlifers), green leafy veg and legumes. We can also afford to eat fewer calories (the World Health Organization estimates that our Basal Metabolic Rate decreases by 2 per cent every decade), so those calories should ideally be good ones: nutrient dense and satiating.

Much of what you'll find in these pages could be described as 'stealth health' – fresh food that tastes so good you'll hardly notice its protective and supportive credentials. The trick is to get these vital building blocks on to your fork in the tastiest way possible, in recipes that make you feel good about eating them, with no denial, no deprivation, no big deal. After all, there's little point in forcing yourself to eat anything you don't enjoy. Better by far to choose foods that really appeal; that, then, is our commitment on every page.

We think of the Midlife Kitchen as an MOT, a time to overhaul and fine-tune your daily diet to access peak performance for the years ahead. It may be that optimum health is your goal, but equally, perhaps you're just bored with the same old meals in your repertoire and want inspiration for interesting recipes that will breathe new life into your cooking. Either way, we hope you find plenty here to spark your appetite.

The Midlife Manifesto

As anyone who reads a newspaper or news feed knows, nutritional advice can be confusing and controversial, particularly at the cutting edge. Rather than promoting the 'clean eating' approach that has recently become fashionable, we want to offer sensible advice, with recipes where you know what you're getting and why. We're naturally wary of buzzwords, so you won't find references to superfoods, detoxing, 'free-from' or restriction. Rather than overpromise, we prefer a simple, assured and – as befits our years – grown-up approach, so we have devised a basic set of guiding principles that we apply when we are creating our recipes:

1.

VARIETY IS VITAL

Restrictive diets aren't just a bore; they reduce gut microbe diversity and can lead in turn to all manner of health issues. In the West, the average person once ate around 150 different foodstuffs; now it's 20, repackaged in 50 different ways. So, our banner is inclusion, not exclusion; a welcome sign, not a 'keep out' notice.

2.

THE WHOLE TRUTH

A balanced diet, rich in fresh produce and low in processed foods and refined sugars, seems to be the most effective long-term health insurance and current best advice, so we aim to maximize the use of natural, whole plant foods in every Midlife recipe.

3.

LESS SUGAR, BETTER FAT, GOOD CARBS

We're well aware that decades of low-fat diet regimes have got us nowhere; obesity, heart disease, stroke and cancer rates haven't responded – so we're looking elsewhere for clues. Good fats (the unsaturated omega-3s, olive oil, coconut oil and, yes, some butter) are very welcome at the Midlife table. The only foodstuff we'd limit is sugar. There's good evidence to suggest that curbing your refined sugar intake and sticking to slow-burn, wholegrain carbohydrates can help control blood sugars and improve insulin sensitivity, which lessens the risk of developing type 2 diabetes. That's one reason why our recipes embrace good grains and slow-burn cereals such as brown and black rice, quinoa and oats. For sweetness, we generally try to stick to fruit sources, date syrup, honey and maple syrup.

4.

TASTE COMES FIRST

Healthy eating must, ultimately, be built upon foods we love to eat, not on those we hate. The point of every recipe in this book – each one honed through experience, experiment and quite a lot of tasty research – is that you'll want to come back for more. (We know. We did.)

5.

EASY DOES IT

While we want each recipe to look and taste wonderful, we also want them to be perfectly doable. We're not in the business of adding to the pressure that already exists around food, so our recipes are purposefully simple, speedy and practical. Midlife is no time to be soaking haricot beans, peeling grapes and stuffing mushrooms. We really have better things to do.

6.

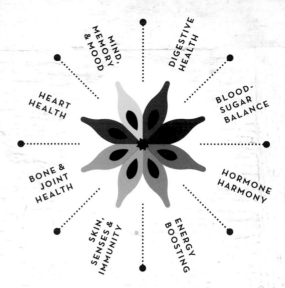

SMALL CHANGES, BIG DIFFERENCE

In developing recipes for the book, we've recognized the importance of 'tweaks' – adding Midlife goodies to familiar recipes to enhance their healthy properties. With that in mind, you'll find 12 Midlife Must-haves on pages 22–35. This is our 'capsule kitchen', a set of store-cupboard essentials to prep in advance and keep on stand-by to make your Midlife Kitchen cooking super simple, super speedy and super tasty. Once you start using them, these essentials will crop up in any number of dishes, and you'll be getting a mega Midlife health boost with every bite.

SOMETHING OLD, SOMETHING NEW

There's nothing too freaky or weird in these pages – in fact, we've gone out of our way to make our recipes comfortably accessible, ensuring that most items are basic, available and that they pass 'the supermarket test'. We want these recipes to become part of your everyday life – a habit, not a one-off where ingredients then languish hopelessly at the back of the cupboard. But if we really believe an unusual ingredient will make a difference to how you feel in midlife, we've included it, with a clear explanation of why it's there. Most items are easy to come by, and those that are less common are listed in the Midlife Larder, see page 14.

HERE'S HOW...

In midlife, health is no longer something peripheral that we can take for granted. It is central to the quality of life that we enjoy. We want all of our recipes to be utterly delicious and full of goodness, so we are wholeheartedly ingredient-led. We have researched the health-giving properties of most of the foods you can think of, plus a few newcomers, too, and cherry-picked the best of these to form the basis for our recipes. For our list of key Midlife ingredients, see our 40+ for 40+ list on pages 16–21.

Nutritional advice does, of course, tend to be in constant flux, with new theories, discoveries and opinions often conspiring to cloud the view (sometimes depending on who is funding the study). At the Midlife Kitchen, we're also sensitive to experiential evidence – for example, where particular ingredients have been used as traditional remedies for generations. We take a pragmatic 'best odds' approach, based on 'weight of evidence': if there is plenty to suggest that an ingredient has certain health benefits and it tastes great, then we think that's a good enough reason to eat it!

Our icon for Midlife health is the star anise, a wonderful spice that has long been used in Asian cooking for its health-giving properties. We have devised a colour-coded system to support and improve health and wellbeing in eight categories, each represented by a star anise seed. If a recipe features that colour seed then it has known benefits in that category. Seeds are awarded for the entire recipe, rather than an individual portion.

Our Star Anise Rating

DIGESTIVE HEALTH

The gut may lack glamour, but – among countless duties – it governs the absorption of vital nutrients and regulates immune function, so keeping our 'gut biome' healthy requires a truly diverse array of foods. At the Midlife Kitchen, we love our guts; that's why you'll find plenty of recipes in these pages incorporating soluble fibre from beans, seeds and oats, spices to aid digestion such as ginger, plenty of leafy greens loaded with vitamins and minerals, bioactive enzymes and probiotics from yogurt and prebiotics from legumes and root vegetables.

The bright red seed shows you where to find recipes which aid digestion.

BLOOD-SUGAR BALANCE

We all know that diabetes has become the major health concern of our age, so it makes sense to eat foods that can help regulate blood sugar and improve insulin sensitivity. These include slow-burn (low Glycaemic Load) carbohydrates from nuts and legumes, soluble fibre from whole grains, oats and seeds, spices known to have anti-glycaemic properties, such as cinnamon, cumin and turmeric, and our Midlife favourite, apple cider vinegar, which can help prevent blood-sugar levels spiking after a meal.

Look for the brick-red seed.

HORMONE HARMONY

Our hormones have far-reaching effects on health – among many other things, they keep our skin supple, our bones strong, our minds alert – and it is age-related hormone imbalance that can lead to common midlife health issues, whether it's flagging energy, low libido, poor sleep or dry skin. The Midlife Kitchen incorporates plenty of hormone helpers; phytoestrogens in foods like soya and flaxseeds, tryptophan in oats and legumes and plenty of good fats in avocados and oily fish. Women, in particular, may need some decent unrefined carbs from whole grains and beans to maintain their endocrine balance.

Look out for the orange seed on recipes that are particularly helpful for hormone harmony.

ENERGY BOOSTING

While our metabolism does gently slow as we get older, if we eat well there is no reason to be 'tired all the time', that common refrain of our age. The link between diet and energy is direct; food is fuel, so it makes sense that consuming foods such as almonds, pumpkin seeds, oats, quinoa, beans, sweet potatoes, yogurt and oily fish – which provide slow, sustaining energy – will help us feel (sometimes literally) full of beans. We also need adequate hydration to maintain energy levels, so drinking plenty of water is essential to feeling more alert and alive.

The blue seed leads the way to increased stamina.

SKIN, SENSES & IMMUNITY

A robust immune system is vital for staving off illness as we age, and we can strengthen our defences by eating fresh foods rich in essential vitamins, minerals and antioxidants. Healthy skin, hair and nails also rely on an adequate supply of vitamins – A (for cell renewal and repair) in carrots, sweet potatoes and spinach; C (for collagen formation) in berries, red peppers and kale; and E (to defend against free-radical damage) in almonds, seeds and broccoli – together with those all-important essential fatty acids from foods like avocados and oily fish. Two groups of plant chemicals – flavonoids and carotenoids – are particularly useful for maintaining supple skin, sharp senses and healthy hair. You'll find them in brightly coloured fruit and veg, which are also great for boosting immunity.

The yellow seed indicates recipes that are particularly beneficial here.

BONE & JOINT HEALTH

In our middle years, due to inevitable hormonal changes, bone density can diminish, so it makes sense that the Midlife Kitchen includes foods containing bone-supporting nutrients. We all know that calcium – from dairy, leafy greens, nuts such as almonds and fish (canned with their bones) – is the building block for bone structure, but we also need vitamin D (in oily fish, butter, egg yolks and mushrooms) to aid its absorption. Our joints can also start to cause us problems as we move into midlife and keeping inflammation at bay is key. Seeds, broccoli, ginger, turmeric and lean protein in chicken, fish and pulses are all important for promoting healthy joints.

Look out for the bright green seed.

HEART HEALTH

Blood pressure and cholesterol levels are critical indicators of health, particularly as we age – and we can give our hearts support by eating foods with a nutrient profile that helps lower both measures. We recommend whole grains, nuts (walnuts and Brazils are excellent), legumes, oats, oily fish, avocados, dark berries, turmeric and loads of leafy veg in the Midlife Kitchen.

The dark pink seed indicates our heart-friendly recipes.

MIND, MEMORY & MOOD

It's essential to maintain cognitive function as we age, and there are plenty of foods thought to help with memory, mood, mental alertness and concentration. Our recipes incorporate many ingredients rich in omega-3 fatty acids or containing specific vitamins, minerals and antioxidants to help keep your brain in tiptop condition. Midlife brain-boosters include oats, nuts, seeds, dark berries, leafy greens, oily fish, extra virgin olive oil, turmeric and dark chocolate (yes!).

Look out for the pale green seed.

WHY US?

Mimi: My early career was spent in London as a fashion journalist for *Vogue*, the *Evening Standard* and then as editor of *ES Magazine*. Once the kids arrived, I moved to Brighton and went freelance, working for national newspapers and magazines, particularly as a columnist for *You Magazine*, *Observer Food Monthly* magazine and *Waitrose Kitchen*. However, I'm probably best known for co-authoring the 2012 bestselling book *The Fast Diet*, which introduced the concept of 5:2 intermittent fasting, and for writing the subsequent recipe books *The Fast Diet Recipe Book* and *Fast Cook*. Those books helped me develop a keen interest in nutrition and health, particularly concerning our changing requirements as the years go by.

Like most people, I've had my health ups and downs: a bout of postnatal depression, a breast cancer scare, a skiing accident that shocked me into realizing I was not invincible, and, more recently, an annoying alcohol intolerance. I still follow the 5:2 Fast Diet from time to time, when I need a weight-loss boost – but these days I'm far more aware of what I eat on non-Fast days, too; my concerns have evolved from a basic desire to watch my weight into something more grounded and, in truth, more vital: the desire to stay really healthy as I grow older. David Bowie, as ever, said it best: 'I think ageing is an extraordinary process whereby you become the person that you always should have been.' Midlife really is our moment. Let's love it and live it well.

Sam: My career so far has taken me from management consultant and travel business owner, to wine buyer and more recently, food writer. As I sit here at my desk in Bali, where I have lived for the past 5 years, I know I have an awful lot to be thankful for. Of course, life has lobbed a few grenades my way: my father died in 2008 from a sudden heart attack aged just 59, and tragically my youngest brother died four years later at 27, from complications arising from type 1 diabetes.

I was in my early forties when the realization dawned that my genetic heritage combined with a lack of attention to my general health was not exactly a recipe for longevity. So, laid up after a minor operation in 2012, I came to the conclusion that what I ate was fundamental to my future health. I wanted to improve my relationship with food and set about doing so. I wrote about the process in *The Happy Eater*, a 4-week programme for those looking to improve their health and bring about sustainable weight loss.

The Midlife Kitchen is the continuation of that food journey. I have found that eating for health can be a fabulous voyage of discovery and an absolute joy. I hope that is what the Midlife Kitchen will be for you: a celebration of delicious and nutritious food that will enable you to grow older vibrantly and vitally.

We are not doctors, chefs or nutritionists. We are regular midlifers, just like you. All nutritional information in the book has been approved by registered dietician and nutritionist Dr Sarah Schenker. If you have a particular medical concern, please consult your doctor. Otherwise, grab a fork and dig in. You'll be doing yourself the world of good.

The Midlife Larder

Most ingredients in our recipes are familiar and will already be on your usual shopping list, but there are some, listed here, which we use in abundance or are just a bit unusual. With these in stock and your Midlife Must-haves to hand, there isn't much in this book that you can't make without the addition of a few fresh ingredients.

BOTTLES

- Light olive oil spray
- Extra virgin olive oil
- Apple cider vinegar ('with the mother')
- Rice vinegar
- Thai fish sauce (nam pla)
- Date syrup or nectar
- Pomegranate molasses

CANS

- Chickpeas
- Butter beans
- Kidney beans
- Black beans
- Coconut milk
- Pumpkin purée
- Peeled cherry tomatoes
- Anchovy fillets
- Sardines

DAIRY

- Natural unsweetened yogurt (see page 20)
- Feta cheese
- Goat's cheese
- Ricotta
- Parmesan

DRIED

- Lentils (green, brown, red, Puy and Beluga)
- White and red quinoa
- Brown basmati rice
- Wholegrain couscous
- Black glutinous rice
- Jumbo oats
- Desiccated coconut
- Medjool dates
- Dried figs
- Apricots
- Cranberries

FROZEN

- Cherries
- Mixed berries
- Blueberries
- Cranberries
- Shelled edamame beans
- Petits pois peas
- Root ginger

JARS

- Cold-pressed coconut oil
- Jalapeño peppers
- Cornichons
- Capers
- Brown rice
- Miso paste
- Tahini
- Harissa paste
- Dijon mustard

MISCELLANEOUS

- Lemons
- Unsweetened almond milk (7%+), see page 296
- Coconut water
- Dark chocolate (minimum 70 per cent cocoa solids)
- Dark chocolate chips or raw cacao nibs
- Date sugar
- Xylitol
- Clear acacia honey
- Nori seaweed sheets
- Sushi ginger
- Vietnamese rice-paper wrappers
- Sea salt flakes
- Matcha (green tea) powder
- Dried hibiscus flowers
- Chai teabags

PACKETS

- Flaxseeds
- Pumpkin seeds
- Sunflower seeds
- Chia seeds
- Sesame seeds
- Almonds (whole, with skin on, blanched, flaked and ground)
- Walnuts
- Brazil nuts
- Cashew nuts
  buy nuts raw and unsalted

READY-COOKED POUCHES

- Lentils
- Quinoa
- Mixed grains
- Brown or red rice

SPICES

- Cinnamon (ground and sticks)
- Cumin (ground and seeds)
- Coriander (ground and seeds)
- Fennel seeds
- Mustard seeds
- Cardamom pods
- Star anise
- Ginger (fresh and ground)
- Nutmeg
- Turmeric (fresh and ground)
- Dried red chilli flakes
- Garam masala
- Vanilla pods (or a vanilla bean grinder)
- Vanilla extract
- Ras el hanout
- Herbes de Provence
- Black peppercorns

40+ for 40+

THE KEY INGREDIENTS FOR MIDLIFE HEALTH

Think of this as your checklist for healthy eating in midlife: just 40 or so ingredients (or ingredient groups) to keep in mind when shopping, cooking or choosing from menus. We've picked each one for the benefits it brings, with particular reference to the health categories designated in our Star Anise ratings. Of course, the list is not exhaustive, but it will give you the basis for a vibrant diet, full of variety and vitality.

APPLES

An apple a day... it's true: apples, fresh or cooked, are a great source of health-boosting antioxidants and pectin, a water-soluble fibre that improves digestive health, lowers cholesterol and helps balance blood sugars. They're also heart-protective and can help guard against osteoporosis, thanks to the boron they contain.

BLUEBERRIES & OTHER DARK BERRIES

We swear by these in the Midlife Kitchen. Blueberries, blackberries and cherries (and cranberries, goji berries and blackcurrants) contain anthocyanins that can help protect against cardiovascular disease, lower blood pressure, improve cognition and memory and support eye health. There's lots of lovely vitamin C in them too, which will boost your immunity. Keep them in the freezer for a year-long dark-berry bonanza.

DATES

A firm fixture in the Midlife Kitchen, dates – particularly the fat, sticky Medjool variety – deliver natural sweetness but have a low GI, so they won't spike your blood sugars to the same extent as refined sugar. Better yet, dates are high in insoluble fibre – great for the gut – and magnesium, which benefits the heart and nervous system.

FIGS

Not just beautiful to behold, figs are also full of good things – including calcium to benefit the bones and fibre to aid digestion. Try them fresh and pink in a salad, or baked in the oven until soft and sticky.

LEMONS & OTHER CITRUS FRUIT

In the Midlife Kitchen, a bowl of (unwaxed) lemons sits right next to the salt and pepper; we consider them the third seasoning and you'll find that many of our recipes involve lemon in some form. Lemons are full of vitamin C, while their plentiful phytonutrients support the heart, immunity and skin health, guard against osteoarthritis and aid iron absorption. Lemon peel contains tangeretin, a phytonutrient that may be effective for helping treat brain disorders such as Parkinson's disease – so add a little zest wherever you can.

POMEGRANATES

Who doesn't love jewel-pink pomegranate seeds scattered on a salad? But they're more than just a pretty ornament – they contain vitamin K for the bones and folate for healthy blood, while plant compounds in pomegranates can prevent oxidative damage to cells and may help lower the risk of diabetes.

VEGETABLES

ASPARAGUS

Asparagus is a Midlife favourite, not only for its unique flavour, but also as a great source of vitamins C and K to keep the skin radiant and the bones strong. It's good for the gut, and is antidiabetic, so will help balance blood sugars.

AVOCADOS

Avocados are indispensable in the Midlife Kitchen. It's all about those heart-healthy good fats, which also enable nutrient absorption from other foods. Avocados are also known to boost immunity, balance hormones, rejuvenate the skin and protect eyesight.

BEETROOT

Brilliant beets crop up time and again in this book – they can benefit the cardiovascular and nervous systems, reduce blood pressure, support the skin, eyes and bones, and help digestive function. They also protect the brain by improving oxygenation.

BROCCOLI

If pressed, we'd choose broccoli as our top Midlife ingredient, thanks to its incredible phytonutrient profile: vitamin C and K, folate, beta carotenoids, sulforaphane, lignans, iron, zinc, phosphorus, calcium, potassium and indole-3-carbinol. Studies have shown that this impressive list will help protect bones, joints, eyes, skin and hair. Broccoli has also been found to enhance brain function, digestion, immunity and energy levels, support the production of red blood cells, lower blood pressure and reduce the risk of many chronic diseases associated with ageing.

CARROTS

It's easy to overlook carrots, but they're brilliantly rich in beta-carotene, lutein, lycopene, potassium and fibre, which means they benefit the heart, digestive system, skin and eyes.

CHILLIES

Chillies not only add glorious heat to many of our recipes, they can also improve mood, thanks to the endorphin-stimulating capsaicin they contain. Chillies have other Midlife powers too, helping to lower cholesterol, steady blood sugar and boost immunity.

FENNEL

Fennel's aniseed bite comes from the aromatic compound anethole, which is a powerful anti-inflammatory. But that's not all: fennel is equally brilliant for your heart, bones, digestion and immunity, as well as for brain and eye function.

GARLIC

Allicin is the wonder stuff here. Found in abundance in garlic, it supports immunity, protects against heart disease and improves blood circulation. There's vitamin B6 too, which boosts the metabolism and benefits the nervous system.

KALE

If you are suffering from 'kale fatigue', give it another try – it's cheap and easy to prep, and it really rates as a health powerhouse. Kale can help lower cholesterol and blood pressure, and it's great for skin, hair and liver function too.

PUMPKIN & BUTTERNUT SQUASH

It's the beta-carotene in orange squash and pumpkin – converted to vitamin A in the body – which is such a bonus for vision and skin. Pumpkin also protects against heart disease and benefits the circulation – all good news in our middle years.

RED CABBAGE

Again, the clue is in the colour: red cabbage is particularly beneficial, thanks to an abundance of anthocyanins, all working to protect the brain, skin and vision; the plentiful vitamins, minerals and fibre in red cabbage will benefit the immune and digestive systems, and help support bone health.

RED ONIONS

We specifically choose red onions over regular white ones because they contain more flavonoids, helping to lower the risk of all manner of age-related diseases. Red onions are also a natural blood thinner, a guard against heart disease and high blood pressure.

RED PEPPERS

Vitamin C, beta-carotene and lycopene are the big hitters here, protecting the eyes, skin and heart, while playing a role in the regulation of blood sugar and blood pressure.

SPINACH

Spinach is an absolute Midlife gift, full of vitamins (C, E, K and Bs) and important minerals such as iron, calcium, magnesium and zinc. So this little leafy green has plenty of clout: it will support bone and tissue health, boost memory, mood and mental agility, and its high fibre content is good for the gut. It also contains carotenoids to benefit the eyes and skin.

TOMATOES

The backbone of the Mediterranean diet, tomatoes are stacked with health-giving goodness; they contain lycopene in abundance, together with vitamin C and plenty of fibre, which is all good news for the heart, bones, gut and skin.

WATERCRESS

Among the most nutrient-dense plants on the planet, and happily available on every supermarket shelf, watercress offers great protection against osteoporosis; it also benefits the brain, lowers blood pressure, improves skin and eye health and can even boost libido.

BEANS

Beans, beans, good for the heart... yes, and they're also brilliant for digestion and blood-sugar regulation. They're a prime plant protein food and an excellent source of sustained energy. Their plentiful B vitamins will help with mood and memory too, making beans a Midlife no-brainer. We use butter beans, kidney beans, pinto beans and black beans – the more the merrier. The darker ones contain antioxidant anthocyanins, which bump up their health credentials.

CHICKPEAS

Full of protein and fibre, chickpeas are an essential (and inexpensive) Midlife ingredient; their mineral content makes them good for the hair, nails and energy levels, and they help stabilize blood sugars too.

LENTILS

We could live on lentils. An excellent protein source, they also support the digestion, hormone system, brain and nervous function, while helping to lower cholesterol and regulate blood sugars. Great in dhals and soups, but we also love them served cold in a salad. Our favourite? Black beluga lentils – it's those anthocyanins again.

SOYA

A complete vegetable protein, soya is known to be protective for your heart and bones, and effective at balancing hormone levels; it contains tryptophan, which supports serotonin production to boost mood, soothe anxiety and promote good sleep. Tofu, tempeh, miso and edamame beans all feature in the Midlife Kitchen.

GRAINS, NUTS & SEEDS

NUTS

The vitamins, minerals, protein, fibre and good fats in nuts make them a simple way to sustain energy and maintain optimum nutrition. Nuts contain tryptophan too, an essential amino acid required for growth and development, and for the production of serotonin, a neurotransmitter thought to enhance sleep and stabilize mood.

Almonds provide fibre and protein as well as vitamin E, which is great for the skin and cellular repair; they're a key non-dairy source of calcium, helpful for maintaining bone density.

Brazils promote heart health by lowering cholesterol levels, while boosting the immune system, enhancing mood and improving memory. Good for the hair, joints, skin and nails – and they increase libido too.

Cashews boost the immune system, keeping eyes, skin and hair healthy. As with most nuts, they're also great for the heart.

Walnuts & pecans help protect against heart disease and age-related cognitive decline; they benefit the skin, can lift mood and have anti-inflammatory properties.

OATS

Oats are so good for the old grey matter that they are known as the 'grain for the brain'; they're also heart-healthy, will boost immunity and are an excellent low GI energy source. You'll find plenty of ways to start your day the oat-y way in our Breakfast & Brunch chapter.

QUINOA

We're keen on quinoa for good reason: it's packed with B vitamins, iron, magnesium, zinc, fibre and protein. With all that going on, it's no surprise that it has multiple health benefits for the brain, digestion, bones and joints; it also helps keep blood sugars steady and could help you sleep well too.

RICE
(wholegrain brown, red, black & wild rice)

Like other whole grains, rice is an excellent source of B vitamins, manganese, magnesium and fibre. It helps regulate blood-sugar levels and aids digestion, and it can also improve memory and mood, aid sleep and lower blood pressure. Not bad for a little grain.

SEEDS

They may be small, but seeds are a potent addition to a diet, thanks to the fibre, vitamins, minerals and omega-3 fatty acids they provide, plus more mood-soothing tryptophan. Scatter them on salads, soups, porridge, yogurt, cakes and puds... or just open a pack and snack.

Chia seeds protect the skin from sun damage and help regulate blood pressure; they contain calcium for healthy bones and fibre to improve digestion.

Flaxseeds are a wonder-seed for midlife: they can ease postmenopausal symptoms thanks to the phytoestrogen they contain. They'll also protect against heart disease, type 2 diabetes and stroke risk, while supporting digestive health, nervous function and collagen production.

Pumpkin seeds are great little energy-boosters with an antidiabetic effect. They also support immunity, heart and prostate health, and promote relaxation and restful sleep.

Sesame seeds are excellent for cellular health, good skin and strong bones and teeth.

Sunflower seeds are known to help protect against heart disease, lower 'bad' LDL cholesterol and stabilize blood-sugar levels.

EGGS, FISH & DAIRY

HERBS

EGGS

For pure nutritional power, nothing beats eggs. They provide vitamins A, D and Bs, plus essential minerals, choline, lecithin and easily assimilated protein. This catalogue of qualities makes them excellent for tissue repair, digestion and heart health, and they'll boost your skin and eyesight. They provide sustained energy and even enhance brain function, concentration and mood.

OILY FISH

It's the omega-3 fatty acids in mackerel and sardines that make them especially good for heart health, reducing fat build-up in the arteries and lowering blood pressure. Oily fish will also help maintain healthy joints, skin, hair and eyesight, guard against bone loss, boost brain function and help circulation. They're also an excellent source of lean protein and can help stabilize blood-sugar levels. A simple tin of sardines would probably be our desert island food.

YOGURT

Plenty of dishes benefit from a good dose of yogurt, and there are convincing reasons to eat it. Recent research has found that people who eat natural unsweetened yogurt every day have a lower risk of developing type 2 diabetes, while it has also been shown to help lower blood pressure. Whole-milk yogurt provides protein, vitamins A, E and Bs, and essential minerals, including calcium, so vital for bone health. Live yogurt, which we heartily recommend, also contains probiotic bacteria (these good guys are not present in heat-treated yogurts), which can enhance immunity, improve vitamin synthesis and assist digestive function.

We use plenty of fresh herbs in the Midlife Kitchen – they're a simple way to bring flavour to a dish, and their phytonutrient content and volatile oils mean they provide a fabulous health kick too.

Basil contains vitamin K to support bone and heart health.

Coriander, a digestive aid, will also help lower blood sugars and LDL cholesterol levels.

Dill strengthens bones and supports the digestion.

Mint is an excellent digestive aid and decongestant, with antiallergenic properties.

Parsley aids oxygenation of the blood, which can help reduce fatigue. Its vitamin K benefits the bones.

Rosemary improves immunity and digestion, and is known to support brain health.

Sage, great for short-term memory, protects the brain, benefits circulation and aids digestion. It can also lower blood glucose and cholesterol levels and help alleviate menopausal symptoms, especially hot flushes.

SPICES

One of the mainstays of Midlife Kitchen cooking, spices bring warmth, colour and flavour to a dish – and they have health-boosting potential too.

Cardamom helps aid digestion and boost immunity and mood; it's also known to lower blood pressure and support bone and cellular health.

Cinnamon helps regulate blood-sugar levels, while supporting liver and gut function, heart health and bone density. It lowers cholesterol, reduces joint pain and can aid sleep.

Cumin is excellent for digestion and can also help with blood-sugar control.

Ginger aids digestion and reduces inflammation (one of the main causes of arthritis). It also lowers the risk of heart disease and type 2 diabetes.

Star anise, anti-inflammatory and antioxidant, is also oestrogenic – so a good hormone helper. It's great for the digestion too.

Turmeric: anti-inflammatory and antioxidant, turmeric is particularly beneficial for the brain and heart; it can help prevent age-related conditions including arthritis, and play a role in regulating blood sugar. Keep fresh turmeric in the freezer until required – just like root ginger.

STORE CUPBOARD

APPLE CIDER VINEGAR

Studies show that apple cider vinegar can help with blood-sugar management, while it also assists calcium absorption and acts as a digestive tonic. We've made it the star of our Midlife Dressing on page 33, but ACV even works as a drink – try our Switchel on page 294 – you'll be pleasantly surprised...

DARK CHOCOLATE

Few of us need any excuse to eat more chocolate, but the dark stuff (70 per cent cocoa solids) provides plenty of health-giving compounds: mineral-rich and high in antioxidants, cocoa is good for the brain, nervous system and heart; it's a mood-lifter too (no surprise there).

GREEN TEA (MATCHA)

Green tea consumption has been shown to lower breast cancer risk in postmenopausal women; it can also benefit the heart and support brain health by enhancing memory and reducing anxiety. It is anti-inflammatory, can improve insulin sensitivity and boost the metabolism. All excellent reasons to go green.

OLIVE OIL

We all know that a Mediterranean diet has significant health benefits – and that's thanks in part to the use of olive oil, which promotes heart health by lowering cholesterol and helping to control blood pressure. It also supports the bones and benefits the nervous system. For a vinaigrette, choose extra virgin, which has more flavour, nutrients and antioxidants than standard oil (keep it in a cool dark place to maintain its freshness). Try a light olive oil spray for quick cooking.

MIDLIFE
MUST-HAVES

WHY WE LOVE IT

We believe spices deserve a far greater role in our cooking – but somehow, for many of us, they seem to languish at the back of a dusty cupboard awaiting an occasional curry. The solution is to make our Midlife Spice Mix in advance and keep it on hand to add instant flavour, depth and a pinch of goodness to all manner of dishes. You'll find this delicious mix cropping up with satisfying regularity in many Midlife Kitchen recipes.

Midlife Spice Mix

MAKES APPROX. 5 TBSP

1 tbsp ground fennel seeds

1 tbsp ground coriander seeds

1 tbsp ground cumin

1 tbsp ground turmeric

2 tsp ground cardamom

Combine all the ingredients and store in an airtight container for up to 6 months.

Midlife Hack: Spices lose their potency (and some of their health benefits) over time, so don't keep them longer than 6 months.

Health Tip
This combination of spices draws on Ayurvedic principles, using turmeric, cumin, coriander, fennel and cardamom to enhance digestion and boost the metabolism. Spices have more recently been proven to have health-boosting antioxidant and anti-inflammatory properties.

WHY WE LOVE IT

The health benefits of seeds are beyond doubt – they're stacked with heart-healthy fats, gut-friendly fibre, mighty minerals, vital vits and energy-boosting protein (seeds, of course, provide the starting blocks for the next generation of plants, so it's not surprising that they are such a complete food). Clearly, these small wonders pack a hefty nutritional punch, but they can often sit in a cupboard, unloved and overlooked. We've found that the best way to introduce more seeds into our cooking is to have a seed mix like this to hand. Add them to wraps, eggs, soups, salads, puds, breads and bakes.

MIND, MEMORY & MOOD

DIGESTIVE HEALTH

HEART HEALTH

BLOOD-SUGAR BALANCE

BONE & JOINT HEALTH

HORMONE HARMONY

SKIN, SENSES & IMMUNITY

ENERGY BOOSTING

Midlife Raw Seed Mix

MAKES APPROX. 9 TBSP

3 tbsp pumpkin seeds

2 tbsp flaxseeds

2 tbsp sunflower seeds

2 tbsp sesame seeds

Combine all the seeds and store in an airtight container for up to 2 months.

Midlife Hack: Because of their high fat content, seeds soak up pesticides, so it's wise to choose organic.

Health Tip
Flaxseeds are a rich source of plant lignans, phytoestrogens that help regulate the body's oestrogen production. This makes them a great Midlife hormone helper (they've even been shown to help reduce hot flushes in menopausal women).

WHY WE LOVE IT

This is a big bang of health-boosting taste and texture to jump-start a salad, soup or wrap. It uses our Midlife Raw Seed and Midlife Spice mixes – so although there seems to be lots of ingredients, it takes mere minutes to assemble and will transform a humdrum bowl of leaves into something spectacular. Try using this mix instead of croutons on soups and in salads.

Midlife Spiced Seed Mix

MAKES APPROX. 8 TBSP

4 tbsp Midlife Raw Seed Mix, see page 25

2 tsp nigella seeds

2 tsp mustard seeds

2 tsp poppy seeds

2 tsp extra virgin olive oil

2 tbsp Midlife Spice Mix, see page 24

1 tsp chilli flakes or smoked/ sweet paprika

sea salt flakes and freshly ground black pepper

Place the raw seed mix in a large, shallow frying pan and dry-fry over a medium heat for several minutes until it starts to colour and pop, adding the remaining seeds for the final minute or so, taking care not to burn them.

Tip the seeds into a bowl and add the oil, spice mix and the chilli flakes or paprika (add more or less according to your liking for heat). Season with salt and pepper.

Transfer the mix to an airtight container and store for up to 2 weeks.

Health Tip
Pumpkin seeds and sunflower seeds contain healthy fatty acids, which can help combat depression and boost your mood.

WHY WE LOVE IT

Australians swear by this homemade mix of ground linseed, sunflower seeds and almonds and it's hard to argue. LSA is a simple and versatile way to catapult omega-3s, protein, minerals, vitamin E and fibre into your recipes, so it makes sense that it's one of our store-cupboard essentials in the Midlife Kitchen. Use LSA as a coating for falafel or simply add it to bakes, smoothies, porridge, yogurt...you name it.

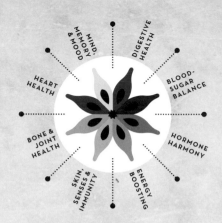

MIND, MEMORY & MOOD
DIGESTIVE HEALTH
HEART HEALTH
BLOOD-SUGAR BALANCE
BONE & JOINT HEALTH
HORMONE HARMONY
SKIN, SENSES & IMMUNITY
ENERGY BOOSTING

Midlife LSA

MAKES APPROX. 12 TBSP

6 tbsp flaxseeds (another name for linseeds)

4 tbsp sunflower seeds

2 tbsp whole almonds (skin on)

Simply use a 3-2-1 ratio of L-S-A. Using a coffee grinder or spice mill, pulse the seeds and almonds in batches until finely ground.

Transfer the mix to an airtight jar and store in the fridge for up to 2 months.

Midlife Hack: It's tricky to buy LSA in the UK – and you're better off making it at home anyway, as the oils shouldn't be heat treated (which would destroy their potency). Due to the high oil content of ground flaxseeds, LSA should be kept in a dark jar in the fridge to prevent it turning rancid.

Health Tip
This combo is rich in antioxidants, vitamin E and a host of good-for-you minerals. Flaxseed is a tough little dude, so it is best consumed in its ground form, which breaks down the shell and releases the nutrients within.

WHY WE LOVE IT

This is porridge with wings – you're getting the usual slow-burn carb-y goodness of oats, but with the added bonus of flaxseeds, almonds, sunflower seeds and oat bran, which turns a very good thing into something truly great. Prep a batch in advance and it will be to hand when you're in a rush and in need of something filling and fast. This is the essence of the Midlife Kitchen: stacking up the health benefits with minimal effort, for maximum taste.

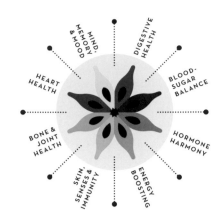

Midlife Power Porridge

MAKES 600G

FOR THE BASIC MIX

400g rolled or jumbo oats

100g Midlife LSA, see page 27

100g oat bran

TO SERVE

125ml milk of your choice
(cow's, almond, soya or oat)
or coconut water (for a lighter
bowl of porridge)

sea salt flakes (optional)

Health Tip
Oats are loaded with dietary fibre, have a range of cholesterol-lowering properties and are also an excellent slow-release energy source, making porridge a brilliant way to start the day.

Combine the basic mix ingredients and store in an airtight container for up to 3 weeks.

To make a simple porridge, place 30g of the basic mix in a saucepan, add the milk or coconut water (we also like to add a pinch of salt) and cook over a low heat for about 5 minutes, stirring frequently, until thickened to your liking.

Try This...
The mix makes a creamy, mildly nutty porridge that works as a comforting base for all kinds of Midlife extras such as:

* Chopped or grated apple and cinnamon, which will boost the antioxidant count of your breakfast bowl
* Banana and Midlife Sweetener, see page 31
* Dried fruits, such as cranberries, raisins, golden raisins, apricots, prunes or goji berries
* Fresh fruit, such as chopped pear, blueberries, raspberries, strawberries, kiwi, mango or cherries
* Canned fruit, such as crushed pineapple, apricots or peaches
* Rhubarb compote or Midlife Apple Sauce, see page 244
* Raw jam, see page 242
* Chopped toasted nuts
* Spices, such as nutmeg, vanilla, grated fresh root ginger, cinnamon or cardamom and a dash of rose water
* Raw cacao nibs

WHY WE LOVE IT

We have a love-hate relationship with granola. We love the delicious nutty crunch it adds to a breakfast bowl, but we hate the fact that most shop-bought versions are stuffed full of sugar. So, in devising this one, we have gone completely sugar-free – a grown-up granola, if you like. Ours still delivers the requisite extreme crunch, but rather than achieving it by baking with masses of oil and sugar, here egg whites do a much lighter and healthier job. Sprinkle on yogurt and add a dollop of raw fruit jam or some dried fruit and you'll have all the sweetness you need.

Midlife Grown-up Granola

MAKES 300G

50g unsalted cashew nuts

100g jumbo oats

50g Brazil nuts, chopped

50g flaked almonds

25g flaxseeds

25g amaranth

1 tsp ground cinnamon

a good pinch of sea salt flakes

3 egg whites

Preheat the oven to 150°C/Gas Mark 2. Line a baking sheet with nonstick baking paper.

Roughly crush the cashews with the back of a spoon, then mix with the remaining dry ingredients.

Whisk the egg whites until stiff peaks form, then add to the dry ingredients, stirring thoroughly with a metal spoon until all the ingredients are fully coated.

Spread the mixture on to the prepared baking sheet and bake for 40 minutes, stirring after 20 minutes to break up the granola a little. Leave to cool completely.

Transfer the granola to an airtight container and store for up to 3 weeks.

Health Tip
Similar to quinoa, amaranth – which means 'everlasting' in Greek – was a staple of the Aztecs. Richer in protein than most other grains, it is also packed with fibre, B vitamins, iron, calcium, magnesium, zinc and omega-3s.

WHY WE LOVE IT

Intensely savoury, deeply nutritious, mildly exotic – this Egyptian dukkah really sums up what the Midlife Kitchen is all about, delivering on taste, texture and versatility with incredibly little effort. Park this in the fridge and reach for it every time you want a flavourful health boost.

Midlife Dukkah

MAKES APPROX. 10 TBSP

2 tbsp whole almonds, blanched or with skins on

2 tbsp pistachio nuts

2 tbsp sesame seeds

1 tsp cumin seeds

1 tsp coriander seeds

1 tsp fennel seeds

10 black peppercorns

10 pink peppercorns

1 tsp sea salt flakes

Place all the ingredients in a large, shallow frying pan and dry-fry over a medium heat for a few minutes until the nuts and seeds start to colour and pop, taking care not to burn them. Leave to cool.

Tip the mixture into a coffee grinder or spice mill and pulse until it resembles the coarse texture of a 'dry rub' seasoning. Alternatively, pound the mixture using a pestle and mortar.

Transfer the dukkah to an airtight container and store in the fridge for up to 1 month.

Try This...
* Sprinkled on soft-boiled eggs or fried eggs, in an egg mayonnaise or as a coating for peeled hard-boiled eggs
* As a topping for salads and soups
* With steamed asparagus, cauliflower, spinach or tenderstem broccoli, or scattered over grilled veggies
* As a rub for chicken or meat, a coating for falafel, folded into hummus or on a baked sweet potato topped with natural yogurt

Health Tip
We add freshly ground black pepper to most of our savoury dishes; not only does it enhance flavour, it also enables your body to absorb more of the nutrients food contains.

WHY WE LOVE IT

We all need a bit of sweetness in our lives, but you'd have to be living under a rock not to know that too much refined sugar is bad news. This is our answer. Yes, dates contain natural sugars, but a little really does go a long way. And, since it's a whole-plant food sweetener, our date syrup is also packed with antioxidants and fibre. Better yet, it takes minutes to make and keeps in the fridge for 3 weeks.

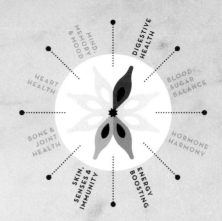

Midlife Sweetener

MAKES APPROX. 10 TBSP

200g pitted Medjool dates

2 tsp lemon juice

300ml water, plus extra if needed

Place all the ingredients in a food processor or blender and process until completely smooth, adding a little more water as necessary – you're looking for something with the consistency of apple sauce.

Transfer to a sealed jar and store in the fridge for up to 3 weeks.

Health Tip
Dates are an excellent source of dietary fibre which, although not considered a nutrient, is required by the digestive system to function properly. Fibre protects against constipation and can help lower blood cholesterol.

WHY WE LOVE IT

An excellent 'semi-salt', this seasoning includes sesame seeds for a shot of added fibre, vitamins, minerals and omega-3 fatty acids. It's a simple combination based on a 1:10 ratio that goes to the heart of what makes the Midlife Kitchen tick: bumping up the health benefits, pumping up the flavour and trying something new that takes mere seconds to prepare. The Japanese call this seasoning *gomashio*; try adding ground nori seaweed sheets to the mix if your taste for umami stretches that far.

Midlife Sesame Seasoning

MAKES APPROX. 4 TBSP

10 tsp black (or white) sesame seeds

1 tsp sea salt flakes

Using a pestle and mortar, pound the sesame seeds until lightly crushed (alternatively, whizz in a blender), then combine with the salt.

Transfer the mixture to a jar and use as an alternative to salt.

Try This...
* On dark green salads
* With French beans
* Sprinkled on an omelette or scrambled eggs

Midlife Hack: Semi-salts can really reduce your salt consumption, while adding dazzling nutrient-rich flavour to any number of dishes.

Health Tip
For such an unassuming little seed, sesame brings quite a lot to the Midlife party: protein, fibre, B vitamins, calcium and iron are just some of their nutrient line-up, guarding against health issues such as high cholesterol and osteoarthritis. They are also a source of phytoestrogens, which can promote the cardiovascular health of menopausal women.

WHY WE LOVE IT

Our go-to vinaigrette: olive oil is the undisputed king of fats – it's heart healthy and can raise the good cholesterol in your bloodstream, while lowering the bad. Choose extra virgin, which has more flavour, nutrients and antioxidants than refined pressings (it tastes more interesting too – grass-green and vivid – which makes it the perfect choice for a vinaigrette). As for apple cider vinegar, choose a raw, unfiltered variety with a recognizable cloudy swirl known, rather fittingly, as 'the mother' – a living ball of enzymes and friendly bacteria.

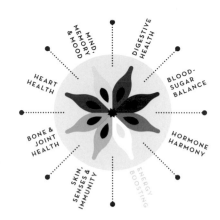

Midlife Salad Dressing

MAKES APPROX. 10 TBSP

4 tbsp extra virgin olive oil

2 tbsp apple cider vinegar

1 tbsp lemon juice

1 tbsp Dijon mustard

2 tsp clear honey

2 tsp dried thyme

sea salt flakes and freshly ground black pepper

Place all the ingredients in a jar, seal with the lid and shake well to emulsify.

The dressing keeps well in the fridge for up to 2 weeks.

Try This...
Our Midlife Dressing works as a great base for other flavours, so try it with:

* A handful each of finely chopped parsley and tarragon for a great green dressing
* A crushed garlic clove, a finely chopped spring onion and a dash of chilli flakes for a punchy version
* Replace the mustard and thyme with 1 tablespoon of tamari and 2 teaspoons of grated fresh root ginger, for an Asian-style dressing
* Replace the mustard and thyme with 1 tablespoon of tahini, 2 teaspoons of sesame seeds and 2 tablespoons of natural yogurt for a creamier dressing

Midlife Hack: Keep extra virgin olive oil and apple cider vinegar in a cool, dark place to prevent them losing potency.

Health Tip
Apple cider vinegar has been shown to have an anti-glycaemic effect, blunting the blood-sugar spike after a meal – reason enough for its starring role in our Midlife Dressing.

WHY WE LOVE IT

This curry paste is called *bumbu kuning*, or 'yellow spice', in Indonesian, thanks to the amount of fresh turmeric root it contains. Blessed with impressive health-giving properties, turmeric has long been used in India to soothe the liver, and in China to treat depression – but in the Midlife Kitchen, we love it equally well for its decadent golden colour and subtle, earthy flavour. This gorgeous, aromatic paste forms the basis of several of our recipes, so it's well worth the bit of contemplative effort required to peel and pulse. As you would expect, it has a southeast Asian vibe rather than an Indian one, so think ginger and lemon grass rather than cumin and curry powder.

Midlife Curry Paste

MAKES APPROX. 10 TBSP

1 star anise

3 cloves

10 small shallots, roughly chopped

15 garlic cloves, roughly chopped

5cm piece of fresh turmeric root, peeled and roughly chopped

5cm piece of fresh root ginger, peeled and roughly chopped

5cm piece of galangal, peeled and roughly chopped

1 lemon grass stalk, tough outer layers removed and thinly sliced

3 kaffir lime leaves, sliced

2–3 hot red chillies, deseeded and sliced, to taste

1 tsp Midlife Spice Mix, see page 24

4 tbsp coconut oil, melted if solid

½ tsp sea salt flakes

freshly ground black pepper

Put the star anise and cloves in a coffee grinder or spice mill and pulse until finely ground. Alternatively, pound using a pestle and mortar.

Tip the ground spices into a food processor or blender, add the remaining ingredients and pulse to a coarse paste.

Store in an airtight container in the fridge for up to 2 weeks.

Health Tip
Turmeric is right up there in the Midlife Hall of Fame, boasting an astonishing array of health benefits. One of the active compounds in turmeric, curcumin, is currently showing promise as a treatment for Alzheimer's disease.

WHY WE LOVE IT

Yogurt is the original A* health food – in fact, full-fat yogurt contains almost every nutrient needed by humans. What you're really after, though, are the clever little bacteria in the live culture. Probiotic literally means 'for life': these microorganisms can help lower cholesterol, improve your immune function and strengthen your digestive system. Taking antibiotics can disrupt the normal balance of bacteria in the gut, as can the menopause or any period of stress – so eating plenty of live yogurt will help rebalance and restore your inner world. Probiotics don't hang around for long, so replenish them regularly by eating yogurt often – it's well worth considering the outlay for a yogurt maker.

Midlife Yogurt

MAKES APPROX. 1 LITRE

1 litre UHT whole milk

2 tbsp skimmed milk powder

2 tbsp live yogurt from previous batch, or shop-bought live yogurt

1/2 tsp vanilla seeds from a pod or a good grind of vanilla bean from a mill, see Midlife Hack on page 211

Place all the ingredients in a large jug and mix together well. Pour into a clean sterilized 1 litre jar or several smaller jars and secure the lid.

Place the jar/s in a yogurt maker and leave to incubate for 8–12 hours, or according to the manufacturer's instructions.

Chill the yogurt in the fridge for a few hours or overnight before serving.

Some tips for successful yogurt making:

* Use jars straight from the dishwasher to ensure they are scrupulously clean
* Using whole milk and adding milk powder will make a super-creamy (though more calorific) yogurt. It will also be higher in vitamin A
* Probiotics are delicate Goldilocks types, so they will only flourish at the right temperature – which is where a maker comes in handy
* If you prep the yogurt in the morning, incubate during the day and chill overnight, it's ready to go for breakfast the following day
* Remember to keep a little yogurt back from each batch to start the next
* After a few weeks of recycling, the taste of your yogurt may become a bit sour and funky; that's when to start afresh with a new shop-bought live yogurt

Health Tip
Recent research has found that people who eat yogurt every day have a lower risk of developing type-2 diabetes, while it has also been shown to help lower blood pressure.

BREAKFAST
&
BRUNCH

WHY WE LOVE IT

We first came up with the idea for *The Midlife Kitchen* at the Yoga Barn in Ubud, eating bowls of this dense, dark rice porridge, so this dish is particularly close to our hearts. Known as 'bubur injin' in Bali, it has a unique silken texture, combines the glories of sweetness and saltiness, and looks fabulously dramatic, especially when coupled with shards of fresh white coconut and the bright orange of tropical fruit.

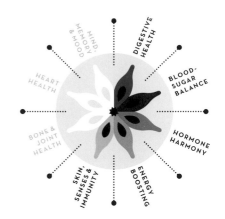

Sweet & Salty Balinese Black Rice

SERVES 4

400ml can coconut milk

150g black sticky rice, soaked overnight and rinsed clean

400ml water

2 tbsp date syrup

½ tsp vanilla extract

sea salt flakes, to taste

TO SERVE

1 mango (or other tropical fruit), peeled, stoned and chopped

1 tbsp finely chopped fresh coconut or desiccated coconut

Reserve 2 tablespoons of the coconut milk and set aside.

Place all the other ingredients in a saucepan and bring to the boil, then reduce the heat and simmer gently for about 30 minutes, stirring often, until the rice is tender, plump and has absorbed most of the liquid.

Serve warm, with the reserved coconut milk and topped with the chopped fruit and coconut.

Try This...
* With blueberries and fresh figs instead of tropical fruit and coconut
* Served with natural yogurt for a black-and-white combo

Midlife Hack: Don't be put off by the prep required – you can buy black glutinous rice from Amazon and other online suppliers, and pre-soaking is not essential, it simply lessens the cooking time. Make plenty, keep it overnight and eat for breakfast the next day too.

Health Tip
Black rice, as you might expect, contains high levels of health-boosting antioxidants called anthocyanins, which are free-radical scavengers, helping to guard against cellular damage.

WHY WE LOVE IT

The very point of porridge is that it's a big hug in a bowl – warming, filling, as comforting as a fairy tale on a dark night. This version ticks all of those boxes and then gives you an additional autumnal cuddle. As you might expect, given their depth of colour, blackberries and black plums have some of the highest antioxidant powers of any fruit. Make this with plain oats, or with our Power Porridge for extra Midlife clout.

Hedgerow Spiced Porridge
WITH BLACKBERRIES, PLUMS, FIGS & HAZELNUTS

SERVES 2

50g Midlife Power Porridge, see page 28, or jumbo oats

250ml shop-bought or homemade unsweetened almond milk, see page 296 (or milk of your choice)

a pinch of sea salt flakes

½ tsp vanilla extract

1 tbsp Midlife Sweetener, see page 31, or 2 tsp date syrup, plus extra to serve (optional)

¼ tsp ground cinnamon

¼ tsp ground ginger

a grating of nutmeg

40g soft dried figs, chopped

40g fresh or frozen blackberries, plus extra to serve

TO SERVE

2 fresh figs, quartered

2 black plums, halved, stoned and sliced

20g hazelnuts, roughly chopped

Place all the porridge ingredients, except the dried figs and blackberries, in a saucepan and cook over a low heat for 3 minutes, stirring frequently, until the mixture starts to thicken.

Add the dried figs and blackberries and gently simmer for a further 2–3 minutes, breaking open the berries to release their juices, until thickened to your liking.

Serve with the fresh figs, black plums and hazelnuts, extra blackberries and a further drizzle of Midlife Sweetener or date syrup to taste.

Midlife Hack: Frozen berries are almost as good as fresh and far cheaper – you can easily buy 'fruits of the forest' mix in most supermarkets.

Health Tip
It's the purple anthocyanins that give blackberries their Midlife badge of honour: dark berries are particularly high in heart-healthy antioxidants.

CARROT CAKE
PORRIDGE

CHERRY CHOCOLATE
PORRIDGE

SPICED PUMPKIN
PORRIDGE

SALTED ALMOND
PORRIDGE

SUPER GREEN
PORRIDGE

WHY WE LOVE IT

Who doesn't adore the comforting taste of carrot cake? This brilliant breakfast take on a classic is super healthy and has no added sugar, with all the sweetness coming from the banana, carrot and sultanas. It maxes out the spices too, so the antioxidant level zooms up.

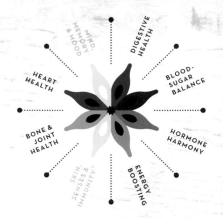

Carrot Cake Porridge

SERVES 2

50g Midlife Power Porridge, see page 28, or jumbo oats

250ml full-fat milk (or milk of your choice)

1 tsp flaxseeds

1 small carrot, about 50g, peeled and grated

½ tsp ground cinnamon

½ tsp ground nutmeg

½ tsp allspice

½ tsp peeled and grated fresh root ginger or ground ginger

2 cardamom pods

1 tsp vanilla extract

½ ripe banana, mashed

20g sultanas

20g goji berries (optional)

a pinch of sea salt flakes

TO SERVE

1 tbsp Midlife Raw Seed Mix, see page 25

a handful of walnuts, chopped (optional)

Place all the ingredients in a saucepan and cook over a low heat for about 5 minutes, stirring frequently, until thickened to your liking.

Remove the cardamom pods and serve with a scattering of Midlife Raw Seed Mix and/or walnuts.

The recipe also works well if you soak the mixture overnight for a super-quick bircher-style breakfast.

See photograph on page 42.

Health Tip
Carrots are brilliant orange because they're high in beta-carotene – a pigment converted to vitamin A in the body, promoting good vision and immune function. Its absorption is improved (up to 6.5 times) if the carrots are cooked.

WHY WE LOVE IT

A pumpkin's gorgeous orange colour is a telltale sign that it's full of health-boosting carotenoids, so adding it to your morning porridge will spike your breakfast with good things. Think of this as an autumnal Thanksgiving special – deliciously warming for a cold day – and the good-carb hit will keep you feeling full for hours.

Spiced Pumpkin Porridge

SERVES 2

50g Midlife Power Porridge, see page 28, or jumbo oats

200ml semi-skimmed milk (or milk of your choice)

100g canned pumpkin purée

1 tsp runny honey, plus extra to serve (optional)

1 tsp finely grated orange zest

1/2 tsp ground cinnamon

1/4 tsp grated nutmeg

a pinch of sea salt flakes

TO SERVE

1 tbsp walnuts or pecan nuts, chopped

1 tbsp pumpkin seeds

1 tsp finely grated orange zest

Combine all the ingredients in a saucepan. Cook over a low heat for about 5 minutes, stirring frequently, until thickened to your liking.

Serve scattered with the nuts, seeds and orange zest, adding a drizzle of honey, if required.

See photograph on page 43.

Midlife Hack: A can of pumpkin works just as well as fresh, and avoids the faff of prep; use the remainder to thicken a root veg soup, or it will keep in the fridge for up to a week.

Health Tip
Pumpkin is incredibly high in vitamin A, which is needed by the body for maintaining good skin and eyesight.

WHY WE LOVE IT

Almonds and cherries are perfect dance partners, and both happen to be key Midlife ingredients. Almonds have been basking in the limelight for a while now and this subtle super porridge uses them in four different forms – milk, butter, extract and flakes – which covers all the bases (the almond butter is calorific, so go easy). Cherries, meanwhile, are bursting with antioxidant power. Keep them in the freezer for a cheap and constant supply.

MIND, MEMORY & MOOD

DIGESTIVE HEALTH

HEART HEALTH

BLOOD-SUGAR BALANCE

BONE & JOINT HEALTH

HORMONE HARMONY

SKIN, SENSES & IMMUNITY

ENERGY BOOSTING

Salted Almond Porridge

WITH WARM CHERRY CHIA JAM

SERVES 2

50g Midlife Power Porridge, see page 28, or jumbo oats

250ml shop-bought or homemade unsweetened almond milk, see page 296 (or milk of your choice)

1 tbsp almond butter

1 tsp vanilla extract

1 tsp almond extract

a pinch of sea salt flakes

1 tbsp flaked almonds, to serve

FOR THE WARM JAM

50g frozen cherries, defrosted

1 tsp chia seeds

First make the jam. Put the cherries and chia seeds in a microwaveable bowl and mash together, then microwave on full power for 2 minutes to make a warm raw jam. Allow to sit while you make the porridge.

Place all the porridge ingredients in a saucepan and cook over a low heat for about 5 minutes, stirring frequently, until thickened to your liking.

Serve the porridge with a dollop of the jam and a sprinkle of flaked almonds.

See photograph on page 43.

Health Tip
Almonds are nutrient dense, high in vitamin E and can assist with blood-sugar control, improve blood pressure and lower cholesterol levels, which is a pretty impressive CV for a little nut.

WHY WE LOVE IT

This is definitely a wild card, but give it a chance – it's packed with Midlife goodies and is unexpectedly delicious. There should be enough sweetness in the ripe banana, but if the green-tea taste is a little strong for you, moderate it with an extra teaspoon of honey to serve.

MIND, MEMORY & MOOD

DIGESTIVE HEALTH

HEART HEALTH

BLOOD-SUGAR BALANCE

BONE & JOINT HEALTH

HORMONE HARMONY

SKIN, SENSES & IMMUNITY

ENERGY BOOSTING

Super Green Porridge

SERVES 2

50g Midlife Power Porridge, see page 28, or jumbo oats

2 tsp runny honey, plus 1 tsp to serve (optional)

1 small courgette, about 40g, grated

a pinch of sea salt flakes

250ml water

1 tsp pure matcha powder

1 small ripe banana, mashed

a handful of blueberries, to serve

Place all the ingredients, except the matcha and banana, in a saucepan and cook over a low heat for about 5 minutes, stirring frequently, until the mixture starts to thicken.

Dissolve the matcha powder in a little boiling water and stir well, then add to the porridge with the mashed banana and heat through.

Serve the porridge topped with the blueberries and drizzled with extra honey to taste.

See photograph on page 43.

Midlife Hack: It's worth hunting down the 'ceremonial grade' Japanese matcha, which is the purest form with the greatest potency. It's an acquired taste, so persevere!

Health Tip
Matcha is loaded with powerful antioxidants that may help lower the risk of heart disease and type 2 diabetes, earning it our vote as the healthiest drink on the planet. Consuming green tea is even thought to enhance memory and reduce anxiety.

WHY WE LOVE IT

If you're having trouble getting your kids interested in porridge, try this unexpectedly healthy chocolate version. You don't even need to tell them that it's packed with gut-friendly fibre and protective resveratrol. Of course, you can eat it too, for all the same benefits.

Cherry Chocolate Porridge

SERVES 2

50g Midlife Power Porridge, see page 28, or jumbo oats

250ml oat milk (or milk of your choice)

1 tsp unsweetened cocoa powder

1 tbsp Midlife Sweetener, see page 31, or date syrup

50g dark chocolate, broken into small pieces

50g fresh or frozen pitted cherries

raw cacao nibs, to serve (optional)

Place the oats, milk, cocoa powder and Midlife Sweetener or date syrup in a saucepan and cook over a low heat for about 5 minutes, stirring frequently, until thickened to your liking.

Stir in the chocolate and cherries and cook for a further 3 minutes until the cherries and chocolate have softened.

Serve the porridge topped with raw cacao nibs.

See photograph on page 42.

Health Tip
Resveratrol, which is found in dark chocolate, is a powerful antioxidant thought to have cardio-protective benefits. Research continues, but we don't need any more persuasion to eat it!

WHY WE LOVE IT

Depth of colour is a clue to the antioxidant power of any fruit or vegetable, so you can tell just by looking at this yogurt combo that it is bursting with health-boosting merit. The pomegranate molasses treads a fine line between sweet and sour, which is just right here – but of course you can use date syrup, honey or maple syrup if you don't happen to have any molasses to hand.

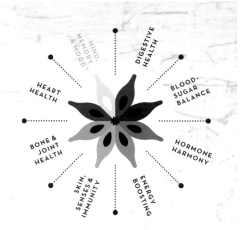

MIND, MEMORY & MOOD

DIGESTIVE HEALTH

HEART HEALTH

BLOOD-SUGAR BALANCE

BONE & JOINT HEALTH

HORMONE HARMONY

SKIN, SENSES & IMMUNITY

ENERGY BOOSTING

Yogurt with Figs & Pomegranate Molasses

SERVES 2

100g natural yogurt

4 ripe fresh figs, quartered

seeds of 1 pomegranate (see the Midlife Hack on page 98 for a quick way to deseed pomegranates)

1 tbsp pomegranate molasses

Divide the yogurt between 2 bowls, then top with the figs and pomegranate seeds.

Drizzle with the pomegranate molasses, grab a spoon and dive in.

See photograph on page 50.

Health Tip
The punicalagins in pomegranates have been shown to reduce inflammation, one of the leading drivers for many age-related diseases.

YOGURT WITH FIGS
& POMEGRANATE
MOLASSES

APPLE STRUDEL
YOGURT

ST CLEMENT'S YOGURT

YOGURT WITH HOT
MEGA-BERRY SAUCE

TROPICAL YOGURT

WHY WE LOVE IT

Here, you get all the delicious flavours of a good strudel – soft apples, fat sultanas, plenty of cinnamon. We've added nuts and dates, increasing the nutrient and energy count to power you through to lunchtime.

Apple Strudel Yogurt

SERVES 2

100g natural yogurt

4 tbsp Midlife Apple Sauce, see page 244, or 1 small apple, grated

1 tbsp Midlife Sweetener, see page 31, or date syrup

1 tsp ground cinnamon, plus extra to serve

2 tbsp walnuts, chopped

1 tbsp flaked almonds

1 tbsp sultanas

1 tbsp Medjool dates, pitted and chopped

Place the yogurt in a bowl and swirl in the apple sauce or apple, Midlife Sweetener or date syrup and cinnamon.

Spoon the mixture into 2 bowls, top with the nuts and dried fruit and a light dusting of cinnamon, then serve.

See photograph on page 50.

Health Tip
We all want to reduce refined and added sugar in our diets, and fruit compotes like apple sauce are a great way to add sweetness in a healthier way. Apples are, of course, high in fibre and vitamin C, but they also contain potassium for heart health and an array of health-boosting antioxidants.

WHY WE LOVE IT

This is a zingy, fresh, fabulous start to the day, banging with vitamin C and rich in calcium from the yogurt and nuts. You can use canned pink grapefruit segments instead of, or as well as, the orange segments to bring even more tang to the table.

St Clement's Yogurt

SERVES 2

1 large orange

100g natural yogurt

1 tsp finely grated lemon zest

1 tbsp pistachio nuts, lightly crushed

a few saffron threads (optional)

1 tsp runny honey

Finely grate the zest of the orange and set aside the zest. Using a sharp knife, remove the peel and pith from the orange, then cut out the segments, removing the membranes.

Divide the yogurt between 2 bowls, then top with the orange segments, orange zest, lemon zest, pistachios and saffron.

Drizzle with the honey and dig in.

See photograph on page 51.

Midlife Hack: Freeze citrus fruits whole, so they're always available to zest.

Health Tip
Lemon and orange peel contains around double the vitamin C of the fruit inside, so don't throw away those skins!

WHY WE LOVE IT

There's something completely irresistible about the combination of tropical fruit, coconut and lime – they somehow add up to an exotic holiday in a bowl. Here, we simply strew these glamour fruits on our thick, creamy yogurt... close your eyes and you can almost feel the sun on your face.

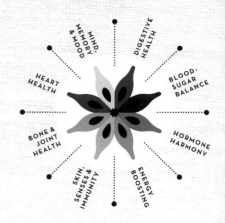

Tropical Yogurt

SERVES 2

100g natural yogurt

1 mango, peeled, stoned and chopped

1 papaya, peeled, deseeded and chopped

1 tbsp chopped fresh coconut or desiccated coconut

1 tsp finely grated or finely sliced lime zest

2 tsp runny honey

Layer all the ingredients, except the honey, in 2 glasses, finishing with a layer of fruit, coconut and lime zest.

Drizzle with the honey and enjoy.

See photograph on page 51.

Health Tip
Papayas contain an enzyme called papain that aids digestion. They are also low in calories compared with most tropical fruit, with just 39 calories per 100g.

WHY WE LOVE IT

This is a dynamite way to eat yogurt – a blissfully rich hot berry sauce, full of health-giving goodies. The pomegranate molasses, date syrup and dark star anise give the sauce a gorgeous, semi-spicy, grown-up flavour. It may be simple, but this would make a great dinner-party dessert, thanks to its complexity of tastes and sumptuous colour.

Yogurt with Hot Mega-berry Sauce

SERVES 2

100g natural yogurt

FOR THE SAUCE
a handful each of fresh or frozen blackberries, blueberries and pitted cherries

1 tbsp pomegranate molasses

1 tbsp date syrup

1 tsp water

1 star anise

Place all the sauce ingredients in a small saucepan and heat through until the berries have burst and released their juice.

Divide the yogurt between 2 bowls, then swirl in the sauce and spoon more on top.

Eat any remaining sauce with a spoon, direct from the saucepan!

See photograph on page 51.

Health Tip
A study of over 16,000 women showed that those eating just one serving of blueberries a week experienced less mental decline over time than those who did not. As they are so delicious, we can't think of any reason why you wouldn't!

WHY WE LOVE IT

Overnight oats are a perfect breakfast if you're in a hurry, and they're a great vehicle for all manner of Midlife brilliance. Here, the classic combo of cherries and chocolate makes for a decadent (and antioxidant) breakfast on the run.

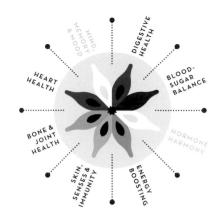

Black Forest Overnight Oats

SERVES 2

100g Midlife Power Porridge, see page 28, or jumbo oats

2tsp chia seeds

2tsp unsweetened cocoa powder

½ tsp ground cinnamon

½ tsp sea salt flakes

300ml shop-bought or homemade unsweetened almond milk, see page 296 (or milk of your choice), plus extra to serve (optional)

½ tsp vanilla extract

2 tsp date syrup

100g frozen pitted dark cherries

large handful of chopped pistachio nuts, to serve

Combine all the dry ingredients in a small Kilner jar or airtight plastic container. Stir in the milk, vanilla extract and date syrup, then top with the frozen cherries. Seal and leave to soak in the fridge for 8 hours or overnight.

In the morning, add extra milk if needed until you get the consistency you like. Add the pistachios and serve.

This can be made up to 3 days ahead and kept in the fridge.

Midlife Hack: Frozen cherries are readily available at most supermarkets, usually for a fraction of the price of the fresh fruit. They generally come ready-pitted too so are super easy to use.

Health Tip
Cherries are very rich in antioxidants, such as anthocyanins and catechins, which can help fight inflammation.

WHY WE LOVE IT

Bircher spends the night in the fridge, where its flavours and textures mingle and develop ready for a speedy, sensational breakfast the next morning. Most traditional birchers include yogurt, which can make them a little rich, but our tropical version uses coconut water to keep it really light.

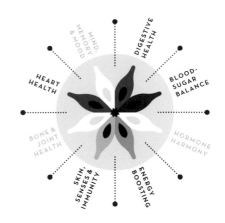

Nurture Bircher

SERVES 2-3

100g Midlife Power Porridge, see page 28, or jumbo oats

250ml coconut water

2 tbsp desiccated coconut

1 tsp finely grated lemon zest

1 small apple, grated

5 pitted dates, chopped

1 tbsp flaked almonds

1 star anise

1 tsp peeled and finely grated fresh root ginger

TO SERVE

passion fruit or other chopped tropical fruit, such as mango, pineapple, melon or papaya

Put all the ingredients, except the tropical fruit, in an airtight plastic container and mix thoroughly. Seal and leave to soak in the fridge overnight.

In the morning, serve topped with tropical fruit of your choice.

Health Tip
Coconut water is great for hydration – indeed, it is often referred to as 'nature's sports drink', replenishing the body with vital nutrients including potassium which helps maintain a healthy balance of fluids in the body.

WHY WE LOVE IT

What's not to love about avocado toast? It's our fall-back breakfast (and lunch... and supper) in the Midlife Kitchen. The trick is to keep the toppings simple but intensely savoury, a foil for the mellow avocado beneath. This version is utterly mouth-watering, with the spiced crunch of the nuts set off by a tang of crumbled goat's cheese or feta.

Nutty Goat Avo Toast

SERVES 2

light olive oil spray

1 tsp Midlife Spice Mix, see page 24

1/2 tsp chilli flakes

50g raw almonds, roughly crushed

sea salt flakes and freshly ground black pepper

4 slices of Seedy Soda Bread, see page 209, or rye or multigrain bread, toasted

1 ripe avocado, peeled, stoned and roughly mashed

100g goat's cheese or feta, crumbled

Heat a small nonstick frying pan and spray with a little olive oil. Add the Midlife Spice Mix, chilli flakes, crushed almonds, salt and pepper and fry for a few minutes until the nuts start to colour, taking care not to burn them.

Top each slice of toast with the mashed avocado, then sprinkle with the nut mix and the cheese.

This works brilliantly with our Zehug (Coriander, Chilli & Tomato Relish), see page 238.

See photograph on page 62.

Health Tip
Avocados contain 'heart-healthy' fatty acids, plenty of fibre and more than 20 essential nutrients; these clever little pears can also boost your body's ability to absorb fat-soluble nutrients from other fruit and vegetables.

WHY WE LOVE IT

This is cheese-on-toast with a twist, but with far less saturated fat than the traditional teatime version. Choose a good-quality seeded bread (try it with our Seedy Soda Bread on page 209) for a guilt-free tower of taste. The basis here, as with any avo toast, is a perfectly ripe avocado – don't even try to get anything glorious from an avocado bullet.

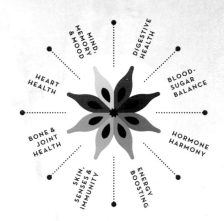

MIND, MEMORY & MOOD

DIGESTIVE HEALTH

HEART HEALTH

BLOOD-SUGAR BALANCE

BONE & JOINT HEALTH

HORMONE HARMONY

SKIN, SENSES & IMMUNITY

ENERGY BOOSTING

Welsh Rarebit Avo Toast

SERVES 2

100g mature Cheddar cheese, grated

2 tsp grainy Dijon mustard

1 tsp milk

a good dash of Worcestershire sauce

4 slices of Seedy Soda Bread, see page 209, or rye or multigrain bread, toasted

1 tomato, thinly sliced (optional)

1 ripe avocado, peeled, stoned and roughly mashed

a grating of nutmeg

Combine the Cheddar, mustard, milk and Worcestershire sauce to form a thick paste.

Top each toast with a couple of slices of tomato, if using, then a quarter of the mashed avocado.

Divide the cheese mix over the avocado and grate with a little nutmeg.

Cook under a preheated hot grill for about 3 minutes until the topping bubbles and starts to brown, then serve.

See photograph on page 62.

Midlife Hack: Keep avocados in the fruit bowl, not in the fridge. If you want one to ripen quickly, place it in a brown paper bag with a banana; both give off ethylene gas, which speeds up the ripening process.

Health Tip
Avocados contain vitamins B, C and K, together with lots of potassium which helps support healthy blood pressure. Studies have also found that eating avocados can significantly improve cholesterol levels.

WELSH RAREBIT
AVO TOAST

NUTTY GOAT
AVO TOAST

SESAME STREET
AVO TOAST

BEANS ON (AVO) TOAST

WHY WE LOVE IT

Here, we've taken avocado toast on a journey to Japan and we think it's a match made in heaven. Sesame and avocado make excellent toast partners, while bean sprouts and thinly sliced spring onions bring a snappy crunch to the deal. If you are a tofu fan you can include some here for extra protein; add a scatter of Midlife Sesame Seasoning and you've got yourself a fabulous, umami-packed start to the day.

Sesame Street Avo Toast

SERVES 2

¼ tsp wasabi paste

1 tbsp tahini

1 tsp sesame oil or extra virgin olive oil

4 slices of Seedy Soda Bread, see page 209, or rye or multigrain bread, toasted

1 ripe avocado, peeled, stoned and roughly mashed

juice of 1 lime

100g tofu, diced (optional)

2 spring onions, finely sliced

a handful of bean sprouts

4 tsp Midlife Sesame Seasoning, see page 32, or sesame seeds

pickled ginger, to serve (optional)

Combine the wasabi, tahini and oil to form a paste, then spread this on each slice of toast.

Top with the mashed avocado, drizzle with the lime juice and add the tofu, if using, the spring onions and bean sprouts.

Sprinkle each toast with the sesame seasoning or seeds and serve with pickled ginger.

See photograph on page 63.

Health Tip
Tahini, made from sesame seeds, is a rich source of B vitamins, which have been shown to boost brain function.

WHY WE LOVE IT

Simplicity is, we've found, the key to avo toast – it should be a tasty, speedy something to rustle up when time is tight. This Mexican-inspired version has the added Midlife magic of fresh tomatoes and pinto beans. Sombrero optional.

Beans on (Avo) Toast

SERVES 2

200g canned pinto beans, rinsed and drained

2 ripe tomatoes, diced

10 jalapeño pepper slices from a jar, diced

4 slices of Seedy Soda Bread, see page 209, or rye or multigrain bread, toasted

1 ripe avocado, peeled, stoned and roughly mashed

2 tbsp natural yogurt

sea salt flakes and freshly ground black pepper

Place the pinto beans in a bowl and mash lightly with a fork. Add the tomatoes and jalapeño slices and mix well.

Top each slice of toast with the mashed avocado, the tomato mixture and a spoonful of yogurt. Season and serve.

See photograph on page 63.

Health Tip
Red beans, such as these pretty, speckled pinto beans, are rich in protein, gut-friendly fibre, antioxidant anthocyanins and slow-release carbs, making them particularly effective in helping to regulate blood-sugar levels.

WHY WE LOVE IT

Chia seeds – tiny, tasteless, ever-so trendy – are also exceptionally healthy, providing protein, fibre, bone-protecting minerals and all-important omega-3 fatty acids. They can (almost miraculously, when you see them for the first time) absorb up to ten times their weight in liquid, producing a gelatinous texture that works brilliantly in combination with fresh fruit or compote for a quick, sustaining breakfast.

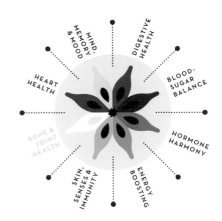

MIND, MEMORY & MOOD · DIGESTIVE HEALTH · HEART HEALTH · BLOOD-SUGAR BALANCE · BONE & JOINT HEALTH · HORMONE HARMONY · SKIN, SENSES & IMMUNITY · ENERGY BOOSTING

Chia-up Pots

MAKES 4 POTS

2 small ripe bananas

300ml shop-bought or homemade unsweetened almond milk, see page 296, or coconut milk

50g chia seeds

1 tsp vanilla extract

Place the bananas in a bowl and mash with a fork. Stir in the milk, then add the chia seeds and vanilla, combining well.

Divide the mixture between 4 small bowls, glasses or ramekins, filling to about halfway.

Chill in the fridge until completely cold, ideally overnight (they'll be fine there for up to 3 days).

Try This...
Top your Chia-up Pots with:

* Chopped strawberries, passion fruit, kiwifruit and orange zest (pictured)
* Chopped mango, strawberries, kiwifruit and mint leaves
* Midlife Apple Sauce, see page 244
* Fresh blueberries and Midlife Grown-up Granola, see page 29
* Raspberries and mint leaves
* Sliced banana and chopped pecans
* Desiccated coconut, pineapple and chopped dates

Health Tip
Chia seeds were prized by the Aztecs and Mayans as a source of sustainable energy (in fact, 'chia' is the ancient Mayan word for 'strength') – and science is now catching up; a recent study found that chia seeds have a stabilizing effect on blood sugar in people with type 2 diabetes.

WHY WE LOVE IT

We ate these gorgeous wraps after a class at the famous Yoga Barn in Bali and knew at once that they warranted a starring role in the Midlife Kitchen, thanks to their fabulous flavour and impressive cast of nutritional goodies. This is definitely a brunch option as it takes a little longer to make than your usual breakfast, but the effort is well worth it. Don't be put off by the egg white bit – we aren't getting all LA on you; an egg white omelette just goes better with the strong pickle and spices. This is best made with our Easy Chapatis (they really are).

Yoga Barn Wraps
WITH GINGER PICKLE

SERVES 2

4 egg whites

1 tsp Midlife Spice Mix, see page 24

a pinch of sea salt flakes

a splash of water

light olive oil spray

FOR THE GINGER PICKLE

1 small carrot, peeled and grated

a thumb-sized piece of fresh root ginger, peeled and finely grated

2 tsp Midlife Sweetener, see page 31, or 1 tsp clear honey

1/2 tsp ground cumin

a squeeze of lemon juice

100ml water

sea salt flakes and freshly ground black pepper

TO SERVE

2 Easy Chapatis, see page 206, or shop-bought seeded wraps

2 tbsp natural yogurt

Place all the pickle ingredients in a small saucepan and simmer for 5 minutes until reduced to a chutney consistency, then set aside to cool for at least 5 minutes.

Using a fork, whisk together the egg whites, spice mix, salt and a splash of water in a bowl until well combined.

Heat a medium nonstick frying pan and spray with a little olive oil to just coat the base. Pour in half the egg mixture and roll it around to thinly cover the base of the pan. Cook for a couple of minutes until lightly golden, then flip and cook on the other side. Remove from the pan and set aside. Repeat with the remaining mixture to make a second omelette.

Place the omelettes on the chapatis or wraps and roll up. Cut each roll in half and serve with Ginger Pickle and yogurt.

Health Tip
We use a lot of ginger in the Midlife Kitchen; among its many health benefits, it is brilliant for the digestion – which explains why ginger is a traditional remedy for seasickness.

WHY WE LOVE IT

We always welcome a new way to eat eggs, as they are nutritionally the best possible start to the day; here, they come in the guise of fluffy, omelette-y mini-muffins. As the base is simply whisked eggs, you can add whatever your taste buds (or your children) desire, but we've done some of the work for you in suggesting a few tasty, healthy power-combos – just choose your favourite and add to the tin.

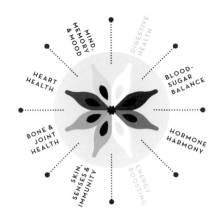

Egg Muffins
WITH AVOCADO SALSA

MAKES 10–12 MUFFINS

light olive oil spray

6 eggs

sea salt flakes and freshly ground black pepper

FOR THE FLAVOUR COMBINATIONS

crumbled feta, olives and finely chopped fresh chilli or chilli flakes

grated Parmesan, finely chopped spring onions and diced tomato

smoked fish (trout, mackerel or salmon), chopped into small pieces, chopped dill and natural yogurt

FOR THE SALSA

1 large ripe avocado

1 spring onion, finely chopped

a handful of flat leaf parsley, chopped

2 tsp lemon juice

1/2 tsp runny honey

Preheat the oven to 190°C/Gas Mark 5. Spray 10–12 holes of a muffin tin with olive oil, brushing each hole to coat really well, then place in the oven.

Whisk the eggs in a jug with a splash of water and salt and pepper.

Take the hot tin out of the oven and pour in the egg mixture to fill halfway up each hole, then top each one with your chosen ingredients. Bake for 20 minutes, or until cooked through and golden.

Meanwhile, peel, stone and dice the avocado, then combine in a bowl with the spring onion and parsley, adding the lemon juice and a little honey to balance the acidity. Season to taste.

Remove the muffins from the oven and leave to cool for a minute or two. Remove from the tray – they may stick a bit so use a palette knife to release the sides. Serve with the avocado salsa.

Health Tip
Eggs contain a little of almost every nutrient we need – vitamins, minerals, protein, healthy fats – and all for a mere 75 calories, making them the perfect Midlife food.

WHY WE LOVE IT

This is one of those dishes that is so much more than the sum of its parts. On the face of it, a comfortingly retro dish of baked eggs, tomatoes and paprika but, with a few Midlife tweaks such as adding peppers and red onions, the antioxidant content is pumped, transforming it into a delicious and nutritious brunch-time feast.

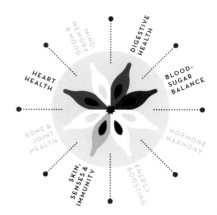

Midlife Shakshouka

SERVES 2

light olive oil spray

1 small red onion, diced

1 garlic clove, crushed

2 small peppers (1 red, 1 yellow), cored, deseeded and chopped

400g can chopped tomatoes

½ tsp chilli flakes, or more to taste

½ tsp ground cumin

½ tsp paprika

½ tsp soft brown sugar

a squeeze of lemon juice

4 eggs

sea salt flakes and freshly ground black pepper

2 tbsp natural yogurt, to serve

a handful of flat leaf parsley, chopped, to serve

Heat a medium-sized frying pan over a medium heat and spray with a little olive oil. Add the onion and sauté for a few minutes until it begins to soften, then add the garlic and continue to sauté for a minute. Add the peppers and cook for a further 5 minutes until softened.

Stir in the tomatoes, chilli flakes, spices, sugar and lemon juice and simmer for 5–7 minutes until the mixture starts to thicken.

Make 4 evenly spaced wells in the tomato mixture, then crack an egg into each one. Season well and cover the pan with a lid. Cook for 10 minutes, or until the egg whites are firm and the yolks still runny.

Serve with the yogurt and scatter with parsley.

Health Tip
Studies have shown that lycopene, a potent antioxidant found in tomatoes, is boosted by cooking, so by slowly simmering this rich, red sauce you are also maximizing the nutritional benefit.

WHY WE LOVE IT

A muffin, we can all agree, is a marvellous thing and these bouncy bran muffins are better yet as they combine plenty of health-giving fibre with very little refined sugar (the sweetness comes instead from date syrup, banana and pineapple). Make a big batch of the mix and it will keep happily in the fridge for up to 3 days – you can add different berries, chopped apple or pear, nuts or seeds to your mix each morning. We've found that they're best straight from the oven on a Sunday morning, eaten warm with a dab of cold butter.

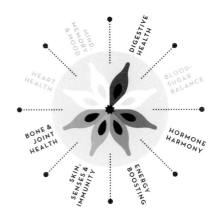

Breakfast Bran Muffins

MAKES 12–16

100g bran flake breakfast cereal

100g wholemeal flour

50g Midlife LSA, see page 27, or ground almonds

100g sultanas

100g canned crushed pineapple

100g natural yogurt

2 eggs

1 tsp ground cinnamon

1 tsp mixed spice

1 tsp ground ginger

1 ripe banana, mashed

1 tbsp olive oil

1 tbsp Midlife Sweetener, see page 31, or date syrup

1 tsp vanilla extract

1 tsp baking powder

a pinch of sea salt flakes

Preheat the oven to 170°C/Gas Mark 3½. Line 1 or 2 muffin tins with paper muffin cases.

Combine all the ingredients in a large bowl and stir well – the mixture will be lumpy.

Spoon the mixture into the muffin cases and bake for 20 minutes until just firm. Eat warm.

Try this...
* Add chopped dried apricots, pitted and chopped dates and top with Midlife Raw Seed Mix, see page 25
* Add frozen berries and ground cardamom
* Add a grated carrot, dried cranberries, and top with oats

Health Tip
Fibre can help reduce the risk of all manner of age-related illnesses, but most of us don't eat nearly enough. A bran muffin is a brilliant way to get your fix.

WHY WE LOVE IT

Once you cook these little beauties, you'll wonder why you didn't discover them years ago. We think of them as pancakes without the guilt trip because they're packed with protein and fibre, and they're also naturally gluten-free. Serve with fresh fruit, spices and seeds for an ideal way to start the day, giving your digestion and energy levels a breakfast boost.

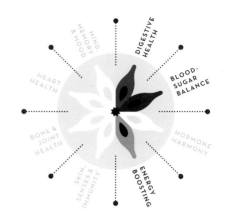

No-flour Banana Pancakes

MAKES 6–8 PANCAKES

2 large ripe bananas

2 large eggs

light olive oil spray

OPTIONAL EXTRAS

1 tbsp Midlife Raw Seed Mix, see page 25, or seeds of your choice

1 tbsp raisins, chopped ready-to-eat dried apricots or other dried fruit

1/2 tsp ground cinnamon

1 tbsp dark chocolate chips (kids love this one!)

Place the bananas in a bowl and mash with a fork, then whisk in the eggs and combine well. Stir in a combination of your choice of seeds, dried fruit, cinnamon or chocolate.

Heat a nonstick frying pan and spray with a little olive oil. Add small scoops of mixture to the pan, enough to make pancakes about 8cm across (if you make them too big they will be hard to flip).

Cook for about 3 minutes on each side until golden and just cooked through.

Try This...

Serve the pancakes warm with your choice of toppings:

* Fresh orange segments, natural yogurt and grated orange zest (pictured)
* A drizzle of maple syrup and chopped papaya
* Grated coconut and chopped mango

Health Tip
Bananas are an excellent source of potassium, a mineral that is essential for heart health, especially blood pressure control.

WHY WE LOVE IT

These are posh pancakes really – so why 'angel cakes'? Well, they're light, fluffy and truly virtuous. The ricotta is less of a taste and more of a texture, making the angel cakes deliciously rich and dreamy. We've chosen to use hemp milk here, just to embrace something new – but semi-skimmed cow's milk would work equally well. This is one for a lazy Sunday: hot coffee, warm angel cakes, fresh fruit, pure heaven.

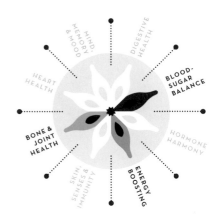

Ricotta Angel Cakes

MAKES 12–15 CAKES

4 eggs, separated

4 tbsp ricotta cheese

2 tbsp Midlife LSA, see page 27, or ground almonds

2 tbsp plain flour

1 ripe banana, mashed

4 tbsp semi-skimmed milk

1 tsp ground cinnamon

1 tsp vanilla extract

1 tsp baking powder

1 tsp maple syrup

a pinch of sea salt flakes

light olive oil spray

Whisk the egg whites in a clean bowl until soft peaks form.

Combine all the remaining ingredients, except the olive oil, in a separate bowl, including the egg yolks (don't worry about a few lumps), then add the whisked egg whites and fold in gently to retain a soufflé texture.

Heat a nonstick frying pan or griddle and spray with a little oil. Ladle on spoonfuls of the mixture and spread them out slightly with the back of a spoon (an 8cm diameter for each cake is about right). When bubbles start to appear, carefully flip the cakes and cook gently on the other side until golden and just set, with a bit of interior wobble. Remove the angel cakes from the pan and keep warm in a low oven. Repeat with the remaining batter.

Try This...
Serve the Angel Cakes warm with your choice of toppings:

* Fresh sliced strawberries, mint leaves, a little extra ricotta and a drizzle of maple syrup (pictured)
* Fresh orange segments and blueberries
* Sliced banana and Midlife Raw Seed Mix, see page 25

Health Tip
One serving of semi-skimmed ricotta cheese provides 67 per cent of the recommended dietary allowance (RDA) of calcium, great for your bones and teeth.

WHY WE LOVE IT

This is a real wake-up in a bowl, a happy salad full of sunshine and good things. Stick to orange and pink fruits to get the prettiest effect. The ginger is the ace card here, elevating it from the mundane to the truly tasty and adding masses of antioxidant power. Use plenty of dressing – the idea is that the fruit should be drenched and the ginger should be strong enough to leave a tingle on the tongue.

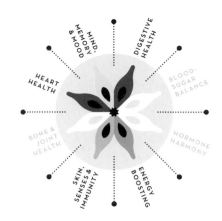

Morning Fruit Salad
WITH GINGER & ORANGE

SERVES 2

orange and pink fruits – enough for 2 people, choose from apricot, nectarine, peach, melon, mango, papaya, guava or orange or pink grapefruit segments, cut into bite-sized pieces

zest of 1 lime, grated or thinly sliced

FOR THE DRESSING

juice of 1 orange

a thumb-sized piece of fresh root ginger, peeled and finely grated

1 tsp runny honey (optional)

2 star anise

Place all the dressing ingredients in a jar, seal with the lid and shake well.

Arrange the fruit in a serving bowl, then add the dressing and sprinkle with lime zest. Serve immediately.

Health Tip
Ginger is a Midlife wonder; not only has it been shown to enhance brain function in midlife women, it also aids digestion and helps lower blood sugars in people with type 2 diabetes.

WHY WE LOVE IT

Smoothie bowls are a bit of a thing at the moment – and there's good reason: not only do they look enticing, they also combine the triple glories of natural yogurt, fresh fruit and satiating carbs to give you a supercharged breakfast. We first spotted this version in a little beach café in Bali and it's just brimming with tropical zing. You can use whatever fruits you have to hand, but do include the coconut flakes and mint leaves – they bring something interesting, tasty and special to the bowl.

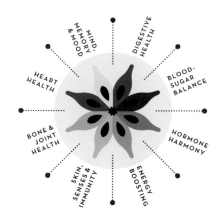

Bali Beach Smoothie Bowl

SERVES 2

10 blueberries

10 strawberries

10 blackberries

3 tbsp natural yogurt

mint leaves, to serve

maple syrup or Midlife Sweetener, see page 31, to serve (optional)

FOR THE TOPPINGS

2 tbsp Midlife Grown-up Granola, see page 29, or muesli

assorted fresh fruit, such as bananas, strawberries, mango and blueberries

2 tsp chia seeds

4 tsp coconut flakes or desiccated coconut

Whizz the berries and yogurt in a blender to produce a smoothie consistency.

Pour the mixture into a bowl, leaving space for the toppings, then line up the granola or muesli, fruit, chia seeds and coconut on the top.

Decorate with mint leaves and, if you like extra sweetness, drizzle with a little maple syrup or Midlife Sweetener.

Health Tip
Desiccated coconut contains a good amount of copper, which supports healthy blood, and manganese, necessary for the activation of important enzymes in the body.

SALADS
&
SOUPS

WHY WE LOVE IT

We love this simple, sparky salad showcasing the healthy lightness that is the hallmark of Japanese cuisine. This makes a perfect lunch alongside a bowl of miso soup; you'll feel full of energy for the rest of the afternoon. *Itadakimasu!*

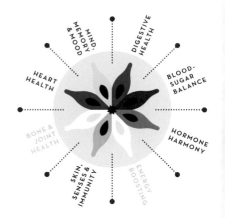

MIND, MEMORY & MOOD

DIGESTIVE HEALTH

HEART HEALTH

BLOOD-SUGAR BALANCE

BONE & JOINT HEALTH

HORMONE HARMONY

SKIN, SENSES & IMMUNITY

ENERGY BOOSTING

Hijuki Salad

SERVES 2

1 large or 2 small sheets of nori seaweed, cut into 1cm thin strips

½ a cucumber, deseeded and cut into thin strips

1 carrot, peeled and cut into thin strips

2 spring onions, thinly sliced

a palm-sized piece of fresh coconut, finely grated, plus extra to serve

25g unsalted cashew nuts, lightly crushed

1 tsp Midlife Sesame Seasoning, see page 32, or sesame seeds, to serve

FOR THE DRESSING

juice of ½ a lemon

1 tsp miso paste

1 tsp soy sauce

1 tsp sesame oil

Put all the salad ingredients into a bowl and combine. (The dressing will soften the nori seaweed, so there's no need to presoak.)

Mix the dressing ingredients and pour over the salad, tossing well.

Divide the salad between 2 large bowls and serve sprinkled with the sesame seasoning or seeds and extra grated coconut.

Midlife Hack: It's worth investing in a 'julienne' tool for making Asian-style salads, where veggies are often prepared in thin strips. It is so quick and lends a pretty look to the dish.

Health Tip
The daily consumption of seaweed is thought to be one of the reasons for a lower incidence of breast cancer among postmenopausal women in Japan.

WHY WE LOVE IT

Possibly the prettiest plate of food you'll ever make. Choose a good, wobbly buffalo mozzarella for the best results – it's the combination of that wobble and the soft, sweet peaches that make this dish such a hit. If you have really sweet summer peaches, there's no need to grill them.

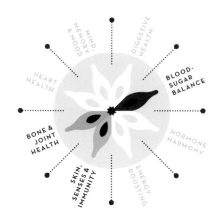

Peach & Mozzarella Salad
WITH PISTACHIO PESTO

SERVES 2–3

2 peaches, stoned and each cut into 8 slices

100g buffalo mozzarella cheese, torn into pieces

a handful of pomegranate seeds

FOR THE PESTO

a handful of basil leaves

a handful of coriander leaves, plus extra to serve

30g pistachio nuts, lightly crushed, plus extra to serve

grated zest and juice of 1/2 a lemon

1 garlic clove, peeled and halved

2 tbsp extra virgin olive oil

sea salt flakes and freshly ground black pepper

Cook the peach slices under a preheated hot grill for 5 minutes until they start to soften and colour. Leave to cool.

Put all the pesto ingredients into a food processor and blitz until almost smooth (you want to retain a bit of texture). The pesto will keep in the fridge for up to 2 days.

Arrange the torn mozzarella and grilled peach slices on a plate and drizzle generously with the pesto. Scatter with the pomegranate seeds, extra pistachios and coriander leaves, then serve.

Midlife Hack: If you find yourself with extra pistachio pesto, keep it in the fridge to have another day with spaghetti, or as a topping for roasted veggies or steamed broccoli.

Health Tip
Peaches are rich in vitamin C, which helps to fight skin damage caused by the sun and pollution.

WHY WE LOVE IT

One of our Midlife mantras is to embrace variety – and the sheer abundance of flavour, texture and colour here will clearly do wonders for you. It's a rainbow of raw excellence, brought together with a terrific tangy dressing guaranteed to transport you to a Koh Samui beach. You'll need a bit of time to chop and slice, but otherwise it's a doddle. Add cubes of tofu or cooked prawns for a more substantial meal.

Raw Pad Thai

SERVES 2

1 small carrot, peeled and cut into thin strips, shaved or shredded

1 small courgette, finely sliced or cut into thin strips

50g red cabbage, very thinly sliced

50g sugar snap peas, sliced

1/2 a pepper (orange, yellow or red), deseeded and thinly sliced

2 spring onions, sliced diagonally

1 mild red chilli, deseeded and thinly sliced

a handful of bean sprouts

a handful of coriander leaves

a handful of mint leaves, plus sprigs to serve

FOR THE DRESSING

2 tbsp coconut milk

finely grated zest and juice of 1 lime

1 tbsp crunchy peanut butter (100 per cent peanuts, no sugar)

2 tsp soy sauce

2 tsp tahini

1 tsp Thai fish sauce (nam pla)

1 tsp sesame oil

1 tsp maple syrup

1cm piece of fresh root ginger, peeled and finely grated

1 garlic clove, crushed

1 lemon grass stalk, tough outer layers removed, finely chopped

TO SERVE

20g peanuts, crushed

2 tsp Midlife Sesame Seasoning, see page 32, or sesame seeds

1 tsp Midlife Spiced Seed Mix, see page 26 (optional)

Place all the vegetables and herbs in a large bowl and mix well.

Place all the dressing ingredients in a jar, seal with the lid and shake well until combined.

Pour the dressing over the salad and toss well, then arrange on a serving plate. Top with the peanuts, seeds and extra mint sprigs and serve.

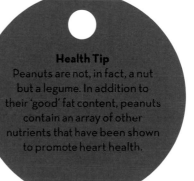

Health Tip
Peanuts are not, in fact, a nut but a legume. In addition to their 'good' fat content, peanuts contain an array of other nutrients that have been shown to promote heart health.

WHY WE LOVE IT

So much more than a salad, this is a veritable taste sensation, thanks to the layering of flavours (sweet, sharp, savoury), textures (creamy, crunchy) and colours (deep ruby reds, pale pinks, vibrant greens). You don't need a huge quantity of Stilton in this salad – regard it as a seasoning rather than a protein fix. The tangy dressing brings the whole lot together for a dish that looks a total treat and requires nothing more for a fabulous lunch.

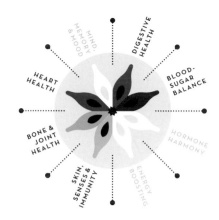

Pink Salad

WITH STILTON CRUMB & POMEGRANATE MOLASSES GLAZE

SERVES 4

2 heads of red chicory, leaves separated

1 small head of radicchio, leaves torn

2 handfuls of baby salad leaves, such as Lollo Rosso and rocket

2 ripe figs, each cut into 8 slices

1 ripe red pear, quartered, cored and sliced into thin crescents

30g walnut pieces

100g Stilton or other hard blue cheese, crumbled

a handful of pomegranate seeds

FOR THE GLAZE

1 tbsp pomegranate molasses

1 tbsp balsamic glaze (or use balsamic vinegar for a sharper dressing)

1 tbsp date syrup

1 tbsp extra virgin olive oil

1 tbsp water

sea salt flakes and freshly ground black pepper

Arrange the salad ingredients, as decoratively as you like, in a lovely serving bowl.

Mix all the glaze ingredients and drizzle over the salad.

Midlife Hack: You can prep all the ingredients in advance and keep in the fridge. Dress the pear slices with lemon juice to prevent browning if you are not serving the salad straight away.

Health Tip
Eating just a small handful of walnuts a day can provide significant levels of the heart-healthy fatty acid ALA (alpha-linolenic acid), which may help to lower 'bad' cholesterol levels in the blood.

WHY WE LOVE IT

This has a little bit of French style and a whole lot of punchy flavour, the leaves functioning as a ferry for a cargo of pure deliciousness. It's ridiculously easy to make and tastes wonderfully decadent, without any undue heaviness, as the blue cheese dressing is moderated with a dollop of yogurt. It's messy to eat, so you'll need a napkin.

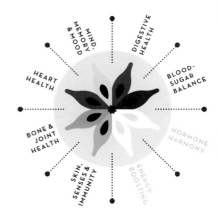

Red Chicory & Walnuts

WITH A WARM ROQUEFORT DRESSING

SERVES 4

2 heads of red chicory, leaves separated

30g walnut pieces

100g Roquefort cheese, crumbled

2 tbsp natural yogurt

Arrange the chicory leaves to sit like boats on a serving plate, then sprinkle the walnuts into each.

Place the Roquefort and yogurt in a small saucepan and heat gently for about 2 minutes, stirring to eliminate the lumps, until it has a soup-like consistency.

Pour the sauce liberally into the chicory boats and eat immediately.

Health Tip
Chicory is rich in phytonutrients, including folate, fibre and vitamins A, C and K; the red cultivar has high levels of antioxidant anthocyanins that can protect the cells that line the gut.

WHY WE LOVE IT

This is just one of those perfect marriages: sweet beetroot, peppery watercress, creamy goat's cheese, the pop of blueberries and the crunch of hazelnuts. It looks pretty as a picture too. Roasting the beetroot slowly will release its gorgeous natural stickiness. We like it with a walnut oil and lemon dressing, which manages to be both delicate and flavourful.

MIND, MEMORY & MOOD · DIGESTIVE HEALTH · BLOOD-SUGAR BALANCE · HORMONE HARMONY · ENERGY BOOSTING · SKIN, SENSES & IMMUNITY · BONE & JOINT HEALTH · HEART HEALTH

Beetroot & Blueberry Salad

WITH HAZELNUTS & GOAT'S CHEESE

SERVES 4

3 raw beetroot (including stems and leaves)

1 tsp extra virgin olive oil

sea salt flakes and freshly ground black pepper

a handful of watercress, thicker stems removed

a handful of salad leaves, such as rocket, lamb's lettuce or mixed baby leaves

1 tbsp hazelnuts, lightly crushed

50g blueberries

50g goat's cheese, broken into small pieces

edible flowers, to serve (optional)

FOR THE DRESSING

1 tbsp walnut oil or extra virgin olive oil

juice of ½ a lemon

1 tsp maple syrup

sea salt flakes and freshly ground black pepper

Preheat the oven to 160°C/Gas Mark 3. Reserve some of the tender beetroot leaves and slice a few of the stems. Scrub the beetroot and cut into 8 or 12 pieces, depending on their size.

Place the beetroot in a small baking tin, drizzle with the olive oil and season with salt and pepper. Bake for about 20–25 minutes until tender. Set aside to cool.

Place all the dressing ingredients in a small jar, seal with the lid and shake well until combined.

Arrange the watercress, salad leaves and reserved beetroot stems and leaves on a serving plate. Add the nuts, blueberries and cheese, then drizzle liberally with the dressing and top with edible flowers.

Health Tip
Don't throw away the leafy tops and slim ruby-red stems of beetroot; they can be steamed or stir-fried or, as here, eaten raw. They are particularly rich in vitamin C, needed for healthy gums, while beetroot leaves also contain iron, folate and beta-carotene, which converts to vitamin A for healthy eyes.

WHY WE LOVE IT

This is a lovely, delicate salad, sophisticated even, but it takes a bit of time and care to properly segment the fruit. Why Pom Pom? Well, pomegranate of course, but the other star of this show is pomelo, which is really just a mega-grapefruit with a slightly firmer texture. It is widely eaten as a snack in Southeast Asia, often with a dusting of salt and sugar; if you have trouble finding one, use grapefruit instead. Here, the citrus tang and sharpness of the fennel and lime are offset brilliantly by the sweetness of the orange juice and pomegranate seeds.

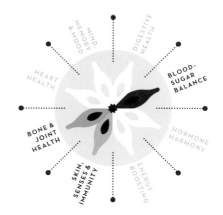

Pom Pom Salad

SERVES 2–3

1 fennel bulb, trimmed and thinly sliced

2 tsp runny honey

2 tsp extra virgin olive oil

1 pomelo or pink grapefruit

100g mixed baby salad leaves

a handful of dill, chopped

seeds of 1 pomegranate, see Midlife Hack

FOR THE DRESSING

juice of 2 limes

juice of 1 small orange

1 tbsp extra virgin olive oil

sea salt flakes and freshly ground black pepper

Preheat the oven to 200°C/Gas Mark 6. Place the fennel on a baking sheet and drizzle with the honey and olive oil. Roast for 15 minutes, or until tender.

Meanwhile, using a sharp knife, remove the peel and pith from the pomelo or grapefruit, then cut out the segments, removing the membranes and place in a bowl with the salad leaves and dill.

Place all the dressing ingredients in a large jar, seal with the lid and shake well until combined.

Pour the dressing over the salad and toss well, then transfer to a serving plate. Top with the roasted fennel and serve sprinkled with the pomegranate seeds.

Midlife Hack: To deseed a pomegranate, cut it in half across the middle. Take each half and hold over a bowl with the seed side down in your palm. Whack the back of the pomegranate with a wooden spoon to release the seeds. Magic!

Health Tip
Grapefruits are full of fibre and skin-supporting vitamin C; eating half a grapefruit before a meal has also been associated with improved insulin sensitivity, which can help lower the risk of type 2 diabetes.

WHY WE LOVE IT

There's something uniquely moreish about salty, squeaky halloumi cheese, and here it's coated in sesame seeds, elevating it to another level of yum. A fennel, lentil and pear base for this salad makes for a substantial meal, packed with Midlife magnificence.

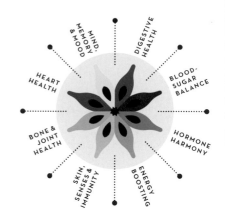

Fenneloumi Salad

SERVES 2

50g dried green or brown lentils or ½ a pouch (about 125g) ready-cooked lentils

1 fennel bulb, trimmed and sliced into 5mm strips

1 tbsp extra virgin olive oil

1 tsp Midlife Spice Mix, see page 24, or ½ tsp ground cumin and ½ tsp ground coriander

sea salt flakes and freshly ground black pepper

juice of ½ a lemon

150g halloumi cheese, thinly sliced

light olive oil spray

a pinch of chilli flakes

2 tsp sesame seeds

1 small Romaine lettuce, shredded

½ quantity of Midlife Salad Dressing, see page 33

1 small pear, cored and sliced

½ a small red onion, thinly sliced

Health Tip
Eating plenty of dairy in midlife means you'll help protect your bones; halloumi, usually made from sheep or goat's milk, is a rich source of calcium and protein. Yes, it's salty too – but because of its robust flavour, a little goes a long way.

If using dried lentils, place them in a saucepan of water and bring to the boil, then reduce the heat and simmer for 25 minutes until tender but still holding their shape. Drain.

Meanwhile, place the fennel in a bowl and coat with the extra virgin olive oil, spice mix or ground spices, salt and pepper. Leave to marinate while you prepare the rest of the dish.

Tip the drained lentils or pouch of lentils into a bowl and dress with the lemon juice, salt and pepper. Chill in the fridge for 15 minutes.

Spray the halloumi slices with a little olive oil, then dust with the chilli flakes and sesame seeds.

Heat a frying pan, add the marinated fennel and cook for about 5 minutes on each side until it softens and colours at the edges. Set aside.

Wipe the pan with kitchen paper to remove any liquid, then dry-fry the halloumi for a few minutes on each side until the sesame seeds are toasted and the cheese is beginning to crisp and brown.

To assemble the dish, toss the lettuce leaves in the Midlife Salad Dressing and place in a serving bowl. Sprinkle the chilled lentils over the lettuce, top with the fennel, halloumi, pear slices and red onion rings. Drizzle with a little more dressing and serve.

WHY WE LOVE IT

There are good Greek salads... and then there are great Greek salads, and this one is packed with health-loving extras. We've added green pepper, cornichons and sunflower seeds for crunch, and handfuls of fresh herbs to give a dear old classic a vibrant update. Make sure your red onion is sliced in almost transparent shards to keep its influence beautifully subtle.

The Mother of all Greek Salads

SERVES 2

½ a head of Romaine lettuce, torn into pieces

10 cherry tomatoes, halved

5cm piece of cucumber, halved and sliced

½ a small red onion, thinly sliced

1 small green pepper, cored, deseeded and thinly sliced

10 Kalamata olives, pitted

10 cornichons, sliced

50g feta cheese, crumbled

a handful each of oregano, mint and coriander leaves

1 tsp Midlife Sesame Seasoning, see page 32, or sesame seeds

2 tsp sunflower seeds

sea salt flakes and freshly ground black pepper

FOR THE DRESSING

1 tbsp extra virgin olive oil

1 tbsp lemon juice

1 tbsp red wine vinegar

1 garlic clove, crushed

1 tsp dried oregano

1 tsp runny honey

Place all the dressing ingredients in a jar, seal with the lid and shake well until combined.

Assemble all the salad ingredients in a bowl and dress liberally, season well with plenty of black pepper and dig in.

Health Tip
Olives contain phenolic compounds that are natural antioxidants and which also give them their distinctive taste. Olives and olive oil may be one reason for lower rates of heart disease and some cancers among those who eat a Mediterranean diet.

WHY WE LOVE IT

Our Midlife Spiced Seed Mix brings a delicious crunch and a whole realm of flavour to an otherwise simple salad. Add the burst of blueberries and a few shards of almond and you have a little bowl of Midlife magic. There's so much going on that you barely need a vinaigrette – just a squeeze of lemon and a hint of extra virgin olive oil and you're done.

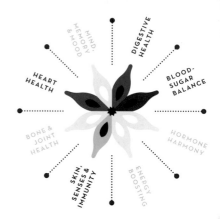

Herb Salad

WITH BLUEBERRIES & SPICED SEEDS

SERVES 2

a handful of salad leaves, such as herbs, rocket and baby spinach

a handful of blueberries

1 tbsp Midlife Spiced Seed Mix, see page 26

2 tsp extra virgin olive oil

juice of ½ a lemon

2 tsp flaked almonds

Place the leaves, blueberries and seed mix in a salad bowl, and toss with the olive oil and lemon juice.

Sprinkle with almonds, then serve and devour.

Health Tip
Blueberries are nature's vitamin tablets: a handful will make a significant contribution to your daily vitamin C and K needs, as well as providing iron, calcium, potassium, magnesium, phosphorus, sodium, manganese, zinc, copper, folate, beta-carotene and choline....Wow!

WHY WE LOVE IT

If we were pressed to name our top Midlife ingredient, a humble broccoli floret would be right up there in pole position; it really is the king of veg, full of mighty vits, minerals and fibre. So broccoli is the rightful star of this crunchy, colourful salad, first eaten at the Cafe Batujimbar near Sam's home in Bali. It's the mix that makes it brilliant, but there's hidden magic too: the mustard seeds will help boost the broccoli's protective health benefits.

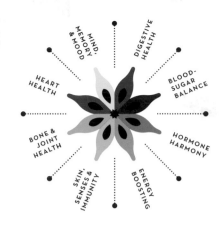

MIND, MEMORY & MOOD

DIGESTIVE HEALTH

HEART HEALTH

BLOOD-SUGAR BALANCE

BONE & JOINT HEALTH

HORMONE HARMONY

SKIN, SENSES & IMMUNITY

ENERGY BOOSTING

Brilliant Broccoli Salad

SERVES 2

1 small head of broccoli, cut in to bite-sized florets; slice the tender stems too

sea salt flakes

50g flaked almonds

100g cooked chilled quinoa, see Midlife Hack

2 tbsp dried cranberries

FOR THE DRESSING

juice of 1 lime

1 tsp runny honey

a thumb-sized piece of fresh root ginger, peeled and finely grated

2 tsp extra virgin olive oil

1 tsp apple cider vinegar

1 tsp mustard seeds

Cook the broccoli florets and sliced stems in a saucepan of salted boiling water for 1–2 minutes. They need to stay crunchy so take care not to overcook them. Refresh in cold water, drain well, pat dry with kitchen paper and set aside.

Heat a frying pan until hot, add the almonds and dry-fry until lightly toasted (this is a very quick process, so do not leave unattended or you will have charcoal flakes). Tip on to a plate and leave to cool.

Combine all the dressing ingredients in a small bowl, stirring well.

Place the broccoli and quinoa in a serving bowl and spoon over some of the dressing. Scatter with toasted almonds and cranberries, finish with a little more dressing and serve.

Midlife Hack: This is an ideal opportunity to bust out a pouch of pre-cooked quinoa; it will save you around 15 minutes cooking time and one less pan in the sink!

Health Tip
A diet rich in cruciferous veg such as broccoli can help reduce the risk of many chronic diseases associated with ageing; broccoli consumption has been linked to reduced risk of cancer and heart disease, as well as improved eye health.

WHY WE LOVE IT

This colour-combo salad is a total taste-fest; with avocado for 'good' fats and black rice for 'good' carbs, it promises to fill you up and give you a satisfying lunchtime energy boost. The recipe features our Spiced Red Cabbage Pickle, so you need to have made this in advance, but it's a delicious Midlife staple that can be kept happily in the fridge for several weeks.

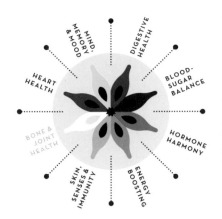

MIND, MEMORY & MOOD

DIGESTIVE HEALTH

HEART HEALTH

BLOOD-SUGAR BALANCE

BONE & JOINT HEALTH

HORMONE HARMONY

SKIN, SENSES & IMMUNITY

ENERGY BOOSTING

RGB Salad

RED, GREEN & BLACK SALAD

SERVES 2

50g black or wild rice, or a 150g pouch of ready-cooked rice (Tilda's Black and Red Lucky Rice is our pouch of choice)

sea salt flakes

1 small avocado, stoned, peeled and sliced

1 small bag (about 90g) rocket leaves

8 radishes, thinly sliced

½ quantity Midlife Salad Dressing, see page 33

6 tbsp Spiced Red Cabbage Pickle, see page 240

freshly ground black pepper

If you're not using a ready-cooked rice pouch, cook the rice in a saucepan of boiling salted water for 20–30 minutes until tender. Rinse under cold running water and drain well. Chill in the fridge for about 15 minutes.

Place the rice, avocado, rocket and radishes in a large bowl, add the dressing and combine well.

Transfer to a large serving plate and top with the Spiced Red Cabbage Pickle and a good grind of black pepper.

Health Tip
Radishes are surprisingly high in fibre. Adding fibre to your diet lowers your risk of diabetes, heart disease and diverticulitis.

WHY WE LOVE IT

We came across the idea of Kale Caesar and, frankly, just loved the name. We found, though, that using only kale was a little too dark and demanding – but it works a treat if you mix half-and-half kale and the more traditional Romaine. The dressing, though rich, is used sparingly; we've added Midlife power by using flaxseed oil (high in polyunsaturated fats), while the anchovies provide a further omega-3 hit. Instead of the usual croutons, we use roasted chickpeas – simple, sassy and full of beneficial insoluble fibre.

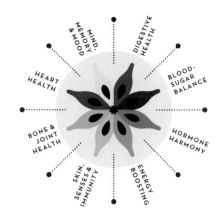

Midlife Caesar

SERVES 4

400g can chickpeas, drained and rinsed

sea salt flakes and freshly ground black pepper

200g kale, tougher stems removed and leaves shredded

200g Romaine lettuce, shredded

30g Parmesan cheese, shaved with a vegetable peeler

FOR THE DRESSING

1 egg yolk

1 tsp Dijon mustard

1 small garlic clove, crushed

2 anchovy fillets, roughly chopped

2 tsp capers, chopped

50ml flaxseed oil

finely grated zest and juice of 1/2 a lemon

freshly ground black pepper

2 tsp water, plus extra if needed

Preheat the oven to 200°C/Gas Mark 6. Place the chickpeas in a baking tin and season with salt and pepper. Bake for 20 minutes until golden and crisp. Leave to cool.

Meanwhile, make the dressing. Put the egg yolk, mustard, garlic, anchovies and capers into a bowl and mix together, then add the oil to the mixture drop by drop, whisking as you go. Add the lemon juice and zest, season with pepper and add a little water to form a coating consistency.

Place the kale and lettuce in a bowl, add the dressing and combine well with your fingers. Transfer to a serving plate, top with the Parmesan shavings and crispy chickpeas and serve. For a more substantial meal, add quartered hard-boiled eggs or sliced, grilled chicken breast.

Health Tip
Flaxseed oil will give your diet a nice little omega-3 boost in the form of ALA (alpha-linolenic acid). The body doesn't process ALA quite as effectively as the fatty acids found in fish and fish oils – but it's still a decent addition to your diet.

WHY WE LOVE IT

Fennel, despite its delicate demeanour, is a truly high-powered vegetable, and a Midlife must: it's stacked with phytonutrients and vitamins that can benefit your bones, blood pressure, heart and immune response. But that's just by the by: the point is that slivers of crunchy, aniseedy fennel, spiked with yogurt, lemon, Parmesan and mint, are a little forkful of joy.

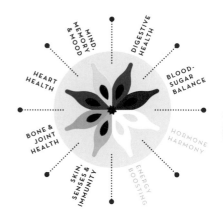

Fennel Carpaccio

WITH LEMON, YOGURT & MINT

SERVES 2

½ a fennel bulb (with fronds)

a handful of small mint leaves

a squeeze of lemon juice

1 tsp extra virgin olive oil

2 tbsp natural yogurt

60g Parmesan cheese, thinly shaved with a vegetable peeler

sea salt flakes and freshly ground black pepper

½ tsp cumin seeds (optional)

Reserve the fronds from the fennel, then trim the bulb and slice very thinly using a sharp knife or a mandoline.

Place the fennel slices on a pretty plate and scatter with some of the fennel fronds. Add the mint leaves and drizzle generously with the lemon juice and olive oil.

Add a drizzle of yogurt and scatter with Parmesan shavings. Season with salt and pepper and, if you like the flavour, a sprinkling of cumin seeds.

Health Tip
Anethole, a component of fennel that provides its distinctive flavour, has been shown to block inflammation; fennel is also known to be great for digestion, thanks to the fibre it contains.

WHY WE LOVE IT

Could this salad be any greener? Or any more delicious? We adore these glistening just-cooked peas, beans and asparagus, shot through with wisps of red chilli, lemon zest and red onion. Yotam Ottolenghi is the inspiration here, but we've added a few Midlife tricks, including skinny, *al dente* asparagus for added oomph. This is one you can prep in advance and assemble quickly, so it makes a great dinner-party showstopper. And, as this salad is leaf-free, it's brilliant for a picnic as it will stay perfectly crunchy even when dressed.

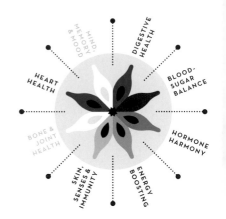

Green Bean & Asparagus Salad

WITH MIDLIFE SPICED SEEDS, TARRAGON & CHILLI

SERVES 4

250g fine green beans, trimmed

250g frozen petits pois

250g mangetout

250g fine asparagus

1 tbsp Midlife Spiced Seed Mix, see page 26

FOR THE DRESSING

2 tsp coriander seeds, crushed

3 tbsp extra virgin olive oil

1 tsp nigella seeds

1/2 a small red onion, finely diced

1 garlic clove, crushed

1 mild red chilli, deseeded and finely sliced

finely grated zest of 1 lemon

a good handful of tarragon leaves, chopped

sea salt flakes and freshly ground black pepper

Cook all the green vegetables in a large saucepan of boiling water until just tender (green beans for 4 minutes, then add the peas, mangetout and asparagus to the boiling water for the final minute). Refresh in very cold water and drain well. Pat the vegetables dry with kitchen paper.

Place the crushed coriander seeds in a small saucepan with the olive oil and heat gently until the seeds begin to pop and release their aroma. Leave to cool, then add the nigella seeds, red onion, garlic, chilli and lemon zest. Leave to stand while you assemble the veggies in a bowl.

Add the tarragon to the dressing and season well. Pour the dressing over the vegetables, sprinkle with the seed mix and serve.

Health Tip
Asparagus is an excellent source of B vitamins, which play a key role in the metabolism of sugars and starches, vital for blood-sugar management.

WHY WE LOVE IT

It's Monday night, the kids are out and you're hungry. In the fridge: a hunk of red cabbage, some radishes. Figs. A lonely jar of pickled baby beetroot and a bunch of dill left over from the weekend pasta. Three minutes slicing and a dollop of lemony yogurt later and you've got yourself a crunchy bowl of salad bliss – sweet, savoury, positively pink with joy and buzzing with antioxidant potential. Lesson? Have good things to hand, recognize happy flavour and texture combinations and don't overthink it.

Red Cabbage Coleslaw

WITH BEETS, FIGS, RADISH & DILL

SERVES 1

50g red cabbage, thinly sliced

8 long radishes, thinly sliced

2–3 pickled beetroot, cut into thin strips

2 ripe figs, each sliced into 4 or 8 pieces

a handful of dill, roughly chopped

FOR THE DRESSING

2 tbsp natural yogurt

a squeeze of lemon juice

2 tsp extra virgin olive oil

sea salt flakes and freshly ground black pepper

Combine the dressing ingredients in a small bowl.

Place the vegetables, figs and dill in a bowl or on a plate, then drizzle with the yogurt dressing.

Eat in front of the telly (optional).

Health Tip
Studies have shown that beetroot, or beetroot juice, can reduce blood pressure by up to 3–10 mm/Hg over a period of a few hours. But don't worry too much about the numbers; if blood pressure is an issue for you, eat beets!

WHY WE LOVE IT

Chris Salans, the inspirational chef behind the beautiful Mozaic restaurant in Bali, gave us this recipe after we visited his café Spice in Ubud. This salad takes a bit of prep, but it's a real show-off dish and the perfect platform for tempeh, a cousin of tofu that has a firmer, and we think much nicer, texture. There is an alchemy that happens here that we can't quite explain; you'll just have to try it for yourself.

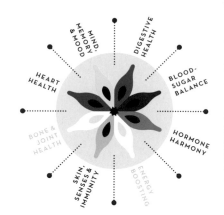

Ubud Spice Salad

SERVES 2

FOR THE SALAD

a large handful of
mixed salad leaves

a small handful of
coriander leaves

1 spring onion,
thinly sliced diagonally

5 radishes, thinly sliced

1 small mango,
peeled, stoned and cubed

1 small avocado, peeled,
stoned and cubed

5 cherry tomatoes, quartered

1 tbsp toasted sesame seeds,
to serve

FOR THE TEMPEH

1 tbsp coconut oil

100g tempeh, cut into 2cm
cubes

sea salt flakes and freshly
ground black pepper

FOR THE DRESSING

2 tbsp Thai sweet chilli sauce

2 lemon grass stalks, tough
outer layers removed, very
finely sliced

2 garlic cloves, finely chopped

2 tsp chopped coriander
leaves (include the plant roots
if possible)

1 tsp Thai fish sauce (nam pla)

a squeeze of lime juice

Arrange all the salad ingredients in a large bowl.

Heat the coconut oil in a frying pan, add the tempeh cubes and fry for about 5 minutes, turning occasionally to ensure the cubes are golden on all sides. Season well and allow to cool slightly, then add the tempeh to the salad.

Combine the dressing ingredients in a separate bowl. Dress the salad and toss to coat (this salad needs plenty of dressing, so don't worry if it seems too much).

Sprinkle with the toasted sesame seeds and serve.

Health Tip
Tempeh is a highly nutritious soya bean product popular in Indonesia and elsewhere in Asia. Unlike tofu, tempeh is fermented, which allows easier digestion of its protein. It contains isoflavones able to mimic some effects of oestrogen, making it potentially beneficial for symptoms of the menopause.

Four Great Salad Dressings

We all have our favourite everyday dressing, the one that lives in the fridge to be called up for duty every time a salad hits the table; you'll find our Midlife version on page 33. But sometimes, a particular combination of salad ingredients demands something creamier, spicier, more complex or exotic. Here, then, are four more super-healthy dressings, each one boasting key Midlife ingredients and guaranteed to make your salad sing.

AVOCADO & TURMERIC

MAKES APPROX. 10-12 TBSP

juice and finely grated zest of 1 lemon

3 tbsp extra virgin olive oil

3 tbsp water, plus extra if needed

3 tsp ground turmeric

1/2 a small ripe avocado

1 garlic clove, crushed

2 tsp runny honey

sea salt flakes and freshly ground black pepper

Put all the ingredients into a food processor or blender and blitz until you have a smooth, pourable dressing, adding a little more water if the dressing is too thick. Store in a sealed jar in the fridge for up to 2 days.

Try This...
* Inside Little Gem 'boats'
* Drizzled on Romaine lettuce leaves
* As a dip for crudités

TAHINI, LIME & CUMIN

MAKES APPROX. 6 TBSP

juice and finely grated zest of 1 lime

2 tbsp tahini (stir well first)

3 tbsp water, plus extra if needed

1 tsp runny honey

1 tsp ground cumin

1 tsp cumin seeds

2 tsp white sesame seeds

sea salt flakes and white pepper

Combine the lime juice, tahini and water in a bowl and whisk until the mixture becomes smoother and creamier. Add the remaining ingredients and stir well. The thickness is up to you – add a little more water if you prefer a runnier dressing. Store in the fridge for up to 3 days.

Try This...
* Poured into half an avocado
* Drizzled over couscous with grilled chicken
* As a dressing for a falafel pitta

The image includes a wheel diagram with the following labels arranged around it: MIND, MEMORY & MOOD; DIGESTIVE HEALTH; HEART HEALTH; BLOOD-SUGAR BALANCE; BONE & JOINT HEALTH; HORMONE HARMONY; SKIN, SENSES & IMMUNITY; ENERGY BOOSTING

CHILLI & HERB

MAKES APPROX. 6–8 TBSP

a handful of coriander leaves, finely chopped

a handful of parsley, finely chopped

1 garlic clove, crushed

1 red chilli, deseeded and finely chopped, or to taste

3 tbsp extra virgin olive oil

juice of 1 lemon

2 tbsp water

1 tsp runny honey

1 tsp sweet paprika

sea salt flakes and freshly ground black pepper

Place all the ingredients in a jar, seal with the lid and shake well until combined. Store in the fridge for up to 3 days.

Try This...
* On a herb leaf salad with grilled halloumi
* As a dip with toasted pitta bread
* Drizzled on warm grilled veggies

MISO, SESAME & GINGER

MAKES APPROX. 6 TBSP

2 tsp miso paste

2 tsp runny honey

2 tbsp rice vinegar

2 tbsp sesame oil

1 tbsp soy sauce

1 garlic clove, crushed

a thumb-sized piece of fresh root ginger, peeled and finely grated

2 tsp black sesame seeds

1 spring onion, white part only, finely sliced

Place all the ingredients in a jar, seal with the lid and shake well until combined. Store in the fridge for up to 3 days.

Try This...
* With Chinese leaf cabbage, pak choi, sugar snap peas, bean sprouts, shredded white cabbage and grated carrot
* As a marinade for fish or chicken
* As a dipping sauce for rice paper spring rolls

Health Tip
An oil-based dressing will make a salad taste great, but research also shows that it can improve the body's absorption of the fat-soluble antioxidant carotenoids in veggies. The same study found that chopping and shredding helps, too.

WHY WE LOVE IT

Peru has recently established itself as a global health-food capital, due to its unique and nutrient-dense array of produce, much of it hauled from the Amazon and the high Andes. This soup includes quinoa, Peru's famous protein-packed super seed, and lean chicken breast; with plentiful coriander, a hint of chilli and a zing of lime, it's a fortifying mini meal in a bowl.

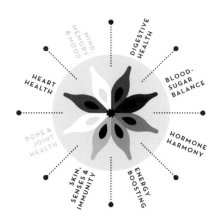

Aguadito

PERUVIAN CHICKEN & CORIANDER SOUP

SERVES 2

50g coriander (leaves and stalks), plus extra leaves to serve

1 small onion, roughly chopped

1 garlic clove, peeled

1 green chilli, deseeded

1 celery stick, roughly chopped

1 tbsp extra virgin olive oil

500ml chicken stock

50g quinoa, well rinsed

1 boneless, skinless chicken breast, about 150g, cut into about 4 pieces

50g frozen peas

juice of 1/2 a lime

sea salt flakes and freshly ground black pepper

lime wedges, to serve

Put the coriander, stalks and all, and the onion, garlic, chilli, celery and olive oil into a food processor and blitz until you get a pesto-like consistency.

Tip the mixture into a saucepan and fry gently for several minutes, then add the stock and rinsed quinoa. Bring to a simmer and cook for 15 minutes.

Add the chicken and cook for a further 15 minutes until the chicken and quinoa are cooked through. Transfer the chicken from the pan to a plate, then shred with a fork. Return the chicken to the pan with the peas and bring to a simmer. Add the lime juice and cook for a few minutes until the peas are tender.

Season and serve scattered with extra coriander leaves and lime wedges on the side.

Midlife Hack: Lazy... but smart: buy ready-diced onion and keep it in the freezer to speed up soup recipes.

Health Tip

Technically a seed but eaten like a grain, quinoa is one of the few plant foods that contains all nine essential amino acids, including lysine and isoleucine acids, which most other grains lack. Naturally high in fibre, quinoa is a slowly digested carbohydrate, making it a great low-GI option.

WHY WE LOVE IT

Forget green juice or anything that tastes remotely of garden clippings, *the* perfect way to get your fill of leafy greens is in a soup – and this is the best we've tasted. Pile in the veg, simmer it down, give it a quick pulse in the blender and there you have it: a delightful bowl of antioxidant goodness. Add a generous spoonful of natural yogurt for a creamy tang.

All-green Soup

SERVES 4

1 tbsp extra virgin olive oil

3 garlic cloves, crushed

5cm piece of fresh root ginger, peeled and sliced

1 tsp ground coriander

5cm piece of fresh turmeric root, peeled and grated, or 1 tsp ground turmeric

1 star anise

sea salt flakes and freshly ground black pepper

500ml vegetable stock

2 courgettes, sliced

1 head of broccoli (including tender stalks), chopped

2 large handfuls of kale leaves (tougher stems removed), chopped

juice of 2 limes

a handful of flat leaf parsley, roughly chopped

2–3 tbsp natural yogurt, to serve

Heat the olive oil in a large saucepan, add the garlic, ginger, coriander, turmeric, star anise, salt and pepper and fry over a medium heat for 2 minutes, then add 3 tablespoons of the stock to add a little moisture to the spices.

Add the courgettes, mixing well to coat in the spice mixture, then pour in the remaining stock, bring to a simmer and cook for 5 minutes.

Add the broccoli, kale and lime juice and simmer for a further 3–4 minutes until all the vegetables are softened (you may have to add a little water depending on the volume of greens, but plenty of moisture will be released from the vegetables).

Remove the pan from the heat and add the chopped parsley. Remove the star anise, then pour the soup into a blender and blitz until almost smooth. Reheat the soup, if necessary.

Ladle the soup into bowls and serve each with a swirl of yogurt and a grind of pepper.

Health Tip
Think of kale as a leafy multivitamin; it can help lower cholesterol and reduce the risk of age-related disease. An 80g serving contains more vitamin C than an orange, and seven times the recommended dietary allowance (RDA) for vitamin K – an important nutrient for bone health and blood clotting.

WHY WE LOVE IT

This super-savoury soup has a great depth of flavour, thanks to the leeks and Parmesan. The Midlife LSA thickens and adds a welcome nutty, nutritious dimension. You can blitz it to a smooth soup or leave it chunkier for a good rustic bowlful.

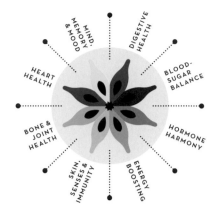

MIND, MEMORY & MOOD · DIGESTIVE HEALTH · BLOOD-SUGAR BALANCE · HORMONE HARMONY · ENERGY BOOSTING · SKIN, SENSES & IMMUNITY · BONE & JOINT HEALTH · HEART HEALTH

Chickpea, Leek & Parmesan Soup

SERVES 4

1 tbsp olive oil

1 tsp butter

2 leeks, trimmed, cleaned and sliced

1 small red onion, diced

2 garlic cloves, chopped

sea salt flakes

400g can chickpeas, drained and rinsed

2 tbsp Midlife LSA, see page 27, or ground almonds

800ml chicken or vegetable stock

freshly ground black pepper

70g Parmesan cheese, grated, plus extra to serve

TO SERVE

a grating of nutmeg

a small handful of parsley, chopped

Heat the olive oil and butter in a large heavy-based saucepan, add the leeks, onion, garlic and a pinch of salt and sauté gently for about 5 minutes until tender.

Add the chickpeas and cook for a further minute, then add the LSA or ground almonds and the stock and simmer for 15 minutes. Season and stir in the Parmesan.

If you prefer a smooth soup, blitz in a blender or use a stick blender. Reheat the soup, if necessary.

Ladle the soup into bowls and add a grating of nutmeg, a scatter of parsley and extra grated Parmesan.

Midlife Hack: Add the rind of the Parmesan to the stock as it simmers to kick up the flavour in this soup. Just remember to remove it before you blitz...

Health Tip
Leeks contain significant amounts of the flavonoid kaempferol, together with plenty of the B vitamin folate and antioxidant polyphenols – all known to protect and support the cardiovascular system.

WHY WE LOVE IT

Hippocrates is thought to have used watercress to treat his patients, and, we now know, with very good reason: this peppery powerhouse contains more calcium than milk, more vitamin C than an orange, and more absorbable iron than spinach. Here's a simple, speedy soup to bring all of that health-giving goodness direct to your spoon.

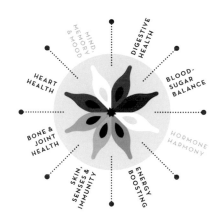

Watercress Powerhouse Soup

SERVES 2

1 tsp butter

1 onion, roughly chopped, or 1 leek, trimmed, cleaned and roughly chopped

1 potato, peeled and chopped

1 bunch of watercress, about 120g, larger stems removed

500ml chicken or vegetable stock

a grating of nutmeg

sea salt flakes and freshly ground black pepper

2 tbsp natural yogurt, to serve

Melt the butter in a saucepan, add the onion or leek and sauté gently for a few minutes until starting to soften. Add the potato and watercress and cook over a low heat for 5 minutes until the watercress has wilted.

Add the stock and nutmeg and season well, then bring to a simmer and cook for about 15 minutes until the potato is tender.

Remove the pan from the heat and blitz the soup in a blender (or use a stick blender) until smooth. Reheat the soup, if necessary.

Ladle the soup into bowls and serve each with a swirl of yogurt.

Health Tip
Recent research has put watercress at the top of the Aggregate Nutrient Density Index, which measures vitamin, mineral and phytonutrient content in relation to calorific content. The sulphur-containing compounds, which give cruciferous vegetables such as watercress their bitter, peppery bite, are also what give them their cell-protecting power.

WHY WE LOVE IT

This soup is a new take on a recipe from Mimi's *The Fast Diet Recipe Book*. It was included there because of its brilliantly low calorie count (around 116 calories per serving), but it's here now on account of its amazing health credentials. It's full of the good stuff – beetroot, apples, star anise, yogurt and seeds – adding up to a rich, warming bowl to fend off the autumn chill.

Beetroot & Apple Soup

WITH STAR ANISE

SERVES 4

500g raw beetroot, scrubbed

1 tbsp olive oil

2 onions, roughly chopped

1 tbsp water

2 Bramley apples

1.5 litres chicken or vegetable stock

2 star anise

sea salt flakes and freshly ground black pepper

TO SERVE

1 tbsp natural yogurt

Midlife Spiced Seed Mix, see page 26 (optional)

Preheat the oven to 180ºC/Gas Mark 4. Place the beetroot on a baking tray standing in 1cm of water. Cook for 45 minutes until tender. Leave until cool enough to handle, then peel and roughly chop.

Heat the olive oil in a heavy-based saucepan, add the onions and the tablespoon of water and cover with a lid. Sweat over a medium heat, without colouring, for about 5 minutes until the onions are softened and translucent.

Peel, quarter and core the apples and add to the pan along with the chopped beetroot. Pour in the stock, add the star anise and season with salt and pepper. Bring to a simmer and cook for 15 minutes until the apples are soft.

Remove the pan from the heat and take out the star anise, then blitz the soup in a blender or with a stick blender until smooth. Reheat the soup, if necessary.

Ladle the soup into bowls and serve each with a swirl of yogurt and a sprinkling of Spiced Seed Mix. A crumble of feta and some chopped flat leaf parsley would be good too.

Health Tip

Beetroot is not just a pretty colour: studies show it can help reduce blood pressure and improve oxygenation to the brain, making it great for mind, memory and mood.

SOTO AYAM

WHY WE LOVE IT

For Sam, one of the many joys of living in a tropical country is the abundance of fresh, fragrant ingredients, which are put to great use in this classic Indonesian chicken soup. In Bali we have this at least once a week and, with your Midlife Curry Paste to hand, it's a doddle to whip up for a quick lunch or light, family-friendly supper.

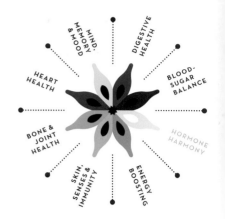

Soto Ayam

BALINESE CHICKEN BROTH

SERVES 2–3

a large handful of coriander (with roots if possible)

1 tbsp coconut oil

1 heaped tbsp Midlife Curry Paste, see page 34

1 boneless, skinless chicken breast, thinly sliced

1 litre chicken or vegetable stock

sea salt flakes

1 large egg

100g mangetout or sugar snap peas

100g broccoli, cut into small florets

a squeeze of lime juice

Rinse the coriander well, then finely slice the roots, if using, and set aside. Remove the leaves from the stalks and reserve a few to serve, then roughly chop the remainder.

Place a saucepan over a medium heat and add the coconut oil, the curry paste and sliced coriander roots and fry gently for a few minutes. Add the chicken and stock and stir well. Bring to a simmer and cook for about 25 minutes until the chicken is tender and cooked through. Taste the soup and add a pinch of salt, if necessary.

Meanwhile, cook the egg in a small saucepan of simmering water for 10 minutes until hard-boiled, then plunge into a bowl of cold water and leave to cool. Peel and quarter the egg.

Add the vegetables, chopped coriander leaves and lime juice to the soup and simmer for a further 2–3 minutes. The vegetables should be *al dente*, so don't overcook them.

Serve the soup immediately, with the boiled egg nestled among the veggies and the reserved coriander leaves scattered over the top.

See photograph on pages 130–1.

Midlife Hack: Much of the flavour in fresh coriander comes from the roots (Asian recipes often use only the roots) so, if you can, buy the whole plant. Wash the roots thoroughly and finely slice.

Health Tip
Coriander is an excellent source of vitamin A – essential for organ function and healthy vision – and vitamin K, important for bone health.

WHY WE LOVE IT

Lentil soup is an absolute health classic, and with our Midlife upgrades in this recipe you'd be hard pushed to pack more nutrition into a bowl. Lentils provide protein, vits and minerals, and are also a great source of 'prebiotics', which fuel the good flora in the gut. Add carrots, onions, garlic and an array of brilliant spices and there's no part of your body that won't feel the sunshine in this sensational soup.

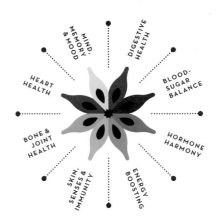

MIND, MEMORY & MOOD

DIGESTIVE HEALTH

HEART HEALTH

BLOOD-SUGAR BALANCE

BONE & JOINT HEALTH

HORMONE HARMONY

SKIN, SENSES & IMMUNITY

ENERGY BOOSTING

Sunshine Soup

RICH LENTIL SOUP WITH MINTY YOGURT

SERVES 2 GENEROUS PORTIONS OR 4 AS A STARTER

1 tbsp olive oil

1 small red onion, finely diced

2 garlic cloves, crushed

3 tsp Midlife Spice Mix, see page 24

2 tsp paprika

1 tsp ground cinnamon

200g canned chopped tomatoes

500ml chicken or vegetable stock

100g dried green or brown lentils, rinsed

2 carrots, peeled and grated

sea salt flakes and freshly ground black pepper

FOR THE TOPPING

a large handful of mint leaves

3 tbsp natural yogurt

a squeeze of lemon juice

Health Tip
Lentils have a low GI and the ability to increase satiety, which means your blood-sugar levels will stay steady and you won't feel like eating for hours after your bowl of Sunshine.

Heat the olive oil in a large saucepan, add the onion, garlic, spice mix, paprika and cinnamon and fry gently for about 5 minutes until the onion is softened.

Add the tomatoes, stock, lentils and carrots, bring to a simmer and cook for 20–30 minutes until the lentils are tender. Depending on how much liquid the lentils absorb, you may need to top up with water if it gets too thick. Season well with salt and pepper.

Transfer the soup to a blender (or use a stick blender) and pulse until fairly thick and coarse-textured. If possible, leave the soup to stand for a couple of hours to let the flavours develop further (or even better, chill overnight in the fridge).

To make the topping, put all the ingredients into a food processor or blender and pulse until the mint is finely minced and the yogurt turns a lovely pale green.

Reheat the soup, then ladle into bowls and serve each with a generous spoonful of minty yogurt on top.

WHY WE LOVE IT

If you have never made miso soup before, now is the time to try. This steaming infusion, gloriously spiked with fresh ginger, is brimming with veggies and delicately poached pale-pink salmon. The fresh cucumber pickle, served here on the side, elevates this Japanese classic to heady new heights: when our friend Nicky told us about this Japanese-style pickle we knew it would be a Midlife winner. Hydrating cucumber, fragrant dill and sharp rice vinegar combine to create a fresh and tangy palate cleanser – the perfect sidekick to any fish dish.

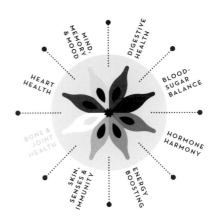

MIND, MEMORY & MOOD

DIGESTIVE HEALTH

HEART HEALTH

BLOOD-SUGAR BALANCE

BONE & JOINT HEALTH

HORMONE HARMONY

SKIN, SENSES & IMMUNITY

ENERGY BOOSTING

Salmon Miso Soup
WITH NICKY'S PICKLED CUCUMBER

SERVES 4

2 salmon fillets, about 125g each

2 tsp soy sauce

1.5 litres water

6 tbsp brown miso paste

a thumb-sized piece of fresh root ginger, peeled and finely grated

4 spring onions, finely sliced

10 mushrooms, quartered

2 carrots, peeled and finely sliced or cut into thin strips

2 heads of baby pak choi, sliced in half lengthways

4 tsp sesame seeds, to serve

FOR NICKY'S PICKLED CUCUMBER

1/2 a cucumber, halved, deseeded and sliced into crescents

2–3 dill fronds, chopped

100ml rice vinegar

1 tsp runny honey

a pinch of sea salt flakes

Health Tip
Miso – essentially fermented soya beans – has been shown to lower cholesterol and is one dietary reason for the low incidence of heart disease in Japan.

To make the Pickled Cucumber, combine all the ingredients in a bowl. Transfer to the fridge and chill for 30 minutes before serving.

Meanwhile, brush the top of the salmon fillets with the soy sauce. Bring 1 litre of the water to a gentle simmer in a large saucepan, then add the salmon fillets and poach for 10 minutes until cooked through, turning once. Remove the salmon from the pan, retaining the cooking water, and leave to cool. Remove any skin and bones from the fish, then flake the flesh into large pieces.

Sieve the poaching water into a clean, large saucepan, discarding any bits. Add the miso paste and ginger and stir until any lumps have dissolved (a mini hand whisk is good for this). Add the remaining 500ml water and bring to the boil.

Add the spring onions, mushrooms, carrots and pak choi, then reduce the heat and simmer gently for about 5 minutes until the veg are tender.

Ladle the broth into bowls, add the salmon flakes and sprinkle with the sesame seeds. Serve with the Pickled Cucumber.

Try This...
Pickled Cucumber is also good served with:

* Swish Rösti with Gravadlax, see page 165
* Fast Falafel, see page 151
* Asian Salad Nori Wraps, see page 182

HEALTHY MAINS

WHY WE LOVE IT

Although this sweet-savoury tagine has an extensive list of ingredients, it really couldn't be simpler – just simmer in a pan for an hour, then ladle over lemony couscous. It's a great one to whip up on a Sunday ahead of a busy week as it keeps well in the fridge (like all of us, its character just improves as time goes by). If you have any left over, blitz it with a little more stock to make a moreish Moorish soup.

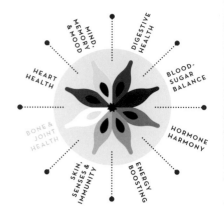

Rich Chickpea Tagine

WITH ORANGE & APRICOTS

SERVES 4

1 tbsp olive oil

1 red onion, thinly sliced

3 garlic cloves, crushed

2 tsp ground turmeric

2 tsp ground cumin

1 tsp ground cinnamon

1 cinnamon stick, broken in two

1 tsp cayenne pepper

1 small aubergine,
cut into bite-sized chunks

2 carrots, peeled
and cut into bite-sized chunks

400g can peeled cherry
tomatoes

400g can chickpeas,
drained and rinsed

75g dried apricots, halved

grated zest and juice of
1 orange

juice of 1/2 a lemon

400ml vegetable stock

1 tbsp honey or date syrup

sea salt flakes and freshly
ground black pepper

200g spinach leaves

a handful of flat leaf parsley,
roughly chopped

FOR THE COUSCOUS

200g wholegrain couscous

a large handful of flat leaf
parsley, chopped

grated zest and juice of
1 lemon

FOR THE HARISSA YOGURT

2 tbsp natural yogurt

2 tsp harissa paste

Heat the olive oil in a large, ovenproof heavy-based pan, add the onion and fry gently for a few minutes until softened, then add the garlic and spices. Cook for 2–3 minutes, adding a splash of water after the first minute or so. Add the aubergine and carrots, stir to coat well in the spiced onion mixture and cook for a further 2 minutes, stirring occasionally.

Add the tomatoes, chickpeas, apricots, orange juice and zest, lemon juice, stock and honey or date syrup. Season with salt and pepper and stir well, then bring to a simmer and cook very gently for 45–60 minutes until the vegetables are tender. Alternatively, bake in a preheated oven, at about 160°C/Gas Mark 3, for 1 hour.

Prepare the couscous according to the packet instructions and leave to stand, then fluff up with a fork. Season with salt and pepper, then stir in the parsley and lemon juice. Sprinkle with the lemon zest.

Add the spinach and parsley to the tagine 5 minutes before the end of the cooking time and simmer until the spinach just wilts. Mix the yogurt and harissa paste in a bowl.

Serve the tagine with the couscous and the harissa-swirled yogurt on the side.

Health Tip
There's a lot to shout about when it comes to chickpeas: they contain protein and insoluble, gut-loving fibre – helping to keep your blood-sugar levels steady and your cholesterol score in check.

WHY WE LOVE IT

Beans are brilliant bolts of goodness: their high protein content + plentiful fibre = top-notch nutrition. Black beans, though, are magic beans, the dark undiscovered pick of the bunch, featuring a host of health-giving quirks that mean they really should feature more heavily in our lives. They also taste wonderful, not unlike mushrooms, with a delicious, velvety texture that demands mopping up with a soft, seedy tortilla wrap. Our promise: you won't be hungry again for hours.

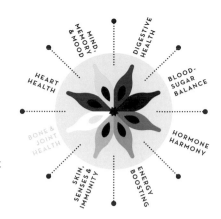

Black Bean Mess

WITH SOFT BAKED EGGS

SERVES 2

1 tbsp olive oil

1 small red onion, finely diced

1 garlic clove, crushed

1 celery stick, finely diced

1 small red pepper, cored, deseeded and finely diced

1 red chilli, deseeded and finely sliced, or to taste

1 tsp smoked paprika

a handful of coriander (leaves and stalks), separated and finely chopped

400g can black beans, drained and rinsed

1 bay leaf

400ml vegetable or chicken stock

sea salt flakes and freshly ground black pepper

2 eggs

TO SERVE

a handful of chopped parsley

2 warm seeded tortilla wraps

Heat the olive oil in a medium frying pan, add the onion and fry gently for several minutes until it starts to soften. Add the garlic, celery, red pepper, chilli, paprika and coriander and cook for a further 10 minutes until everything softens.

Add the black beans, bay leaf and stock. Stir, bring to a simmer and cook for 30–35 minutes until thickened. Remove the pan from the heat and mash the beans a little with a fork (aim for the consistency of a thick dhal).

Season and stir, then make 2 wells in the mixture. Crack an egg into each hollow, cover the pan with a lid and cook over a medium heat for a further 3–4 minutes, or until the eggs are cooked to your liking.

Scatter with the parsley and serve with warm tortillas.

Health Tip
Black beans are high in phytonutrient anthocyanins, those all-important antioxidants that can help guard against disease. In fact, they have more antioxidant activity, gram for gram, than other beans.

WHY WE LOVE IT

The idea of digging into a big bowl of soulfood may seem a bit trendy, but it's a great, no-fuss way to get a balanced burst of slow-burn carbs, lots of veggies and just enough protein in every bite. This first Nourish Bowl (there are 2 more on the following pages) has got the lot: sweet, nutty, earthy...there's plenty going on here, with very little effort. We're all pressed for time, so the 'shove it in the oven' approach rules in the Midlife Kitchen!

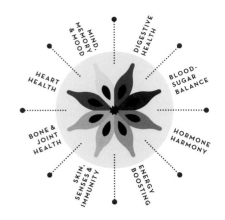

Butternut, Butter Bean & Red Onion Roast

WITH FETA & PINE NUTS

SERVES 2

350g bag ready-diced butternut squash and sweet potato

1 large red onion, cut into 8 wedges

6 garlic cloves, peeled

a squeeze of lemon juice

sea salt flakes and freshly ground black pepper

2 tbsp olive oil

400g can butter beans, drained and rinsed

TO SERVE

a small handful of thyme, leaves picked and chopped

50g feta cheese, crumbled

2 tbsp toasted pine nuts

a handful of pomegranate seeds

Preheat the oven to 190°C/Gas Mark 5.

Place the squash, sweet potato, onion, garlic and lemon juice in a roasting tin, season with salt and pepper and drizzle with the olive oil. Bake for 40 minutes until softened and starting to caramelize.

Add the butter beans, giving everything a shove around with a wooden spoon to release the sticky bits. Return to the oven and bake for a further 5–10 minutes.

Divide between 2 bowls and serve sprinkled with the thyme, feta, toasted pine nuts and pomegranate seeds.

Midlife Hack: If there are any leftovers, this mix makes a great soup. Just add stock, blend, heat and serve.

Health Tip
Garlic has a raft of health-giving properties that can benefit midlifers – in particular, it can help lower blood pressure and cholesterol levels for improved heart health.

ROASTED BEETROOT WITH
SPICED ORANGE, RAS EL HANOUT
& GOAT'S CHEESE

BUTTERNUT, BUTTER BEAN
AND RED ONION ROAST
WITH FETA & PINE NUTS

ROASTED PUMPKIN WITH
QUINOA & LABNEH

WHY WE LOVE IT

'Ras el hanout' is Arabic for 'head of the shop', suggesting a mixture of the best spices a seller has to offer. Well, we're all about spices here in the Midlife Kitchen, and this aromatic, antioxidant North African blend works wonderfully with the sticky beetroot, sweet carrot and curls of roasted red onion in this sublime bowlful. You'll get a little protein and dairy dynamite from the goat's cheese too. The mint isn't just for show: it brings another layer of lovely to the dish.

Roasted Beetroot

WITH SPICED ORANGE, RAS EL HANOUT & GOAT'S CHEESE

SERVES 2

1 large carrot, peeled and cut into batons

4 ready-cooked beetroot, about 250g in total, halved or quartered

1 red onion, cut into 8 wedges

juice of 1 orange

2 tbsp olive oil

sea salt flakes and freshly ground black pepper

1 tbsp ras el hanout

1 tsp cumin seeds

TO SERVE

1 carrot, peeled and shaved into ribbons

a handful of mint leaves

50g goat's cheese, crumbled

Preheat the oven to 200°C/Gas Mark 6.

Place the carrot batons, beetroot and red onion in a roasting tin and add the orange juice and olive oil. Season well and sprinkle with the ras el hanout and cumin seeds. Bake for 40 minutes until the vegetables are softened and sticky.

Divide the roasted veg, either warm or at room temperature, between 2 ample bowls, then add the shaved carrot ribbons, scatter with the mint and top with the goat's cheese.

See photograph on page 143.

Health Tip
A recent study found that beetroot can help slow the progression of dementia in older adults.

WHY WE LOVE IT

Pumpkin is a storehouse of vitamins, minerals, fibre and antioxidants, so it made sense to give it the starring role in this gathering of the glorious, the great and the good. Almost every ingredient in this brilliant bowl is a Midlife winner. If you haven't made labneh before, give it a go – it's a simple, strained, garlicky yogurt that hails from the Middle East and it really brings something special to the show here. Otherwise, a little crushed garlic mixed with yogurt makes a great understudy.

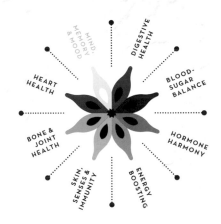

Roasted Pumpkin

WITH QUINOA & LABNEH

SERVES 4

1 tbsp olive oil

2cm piece of fresh root ginger, peeled and grated

2 tsp ground cinnamon

1 tsp chilli flakes

500g pumpkin, peeled, deseeded and sliced into 3cm pieces

1 red onion, cut into 8 wedges

sea salt flakes and freshly ground black pepper

2 tsp maple syrup

a squeeze of lemon juice

2 tsp Midlife Sesame Seasoning, see page 32, or black sesame seeds

a handful of baby spinach leaves and/or baby watercress

a handful of coriander leaves, roughly chopped

a handful of mint leaves, roughly chopped

20 cherry tomatoes, halved

250g pouch ready-cooked quinoa

50g walnuts, chopped

30g pumpkin seeds

FOR THE DRESSING

3 tbsp extra virgin olive oil

2 tbsp apple cider vinegar

1 tbsp pomegranate molasses

2 tsp date syrup

1 tsp Dijon mustard

juice of 1/2 a lemon

FOR THE LABNEH

150g thick Greek yogurt

1 garlic clove, crushed

2 tsp cumin seeds

sea salt flakes and freshly ground black pepper

To make the labneh, strain the yogurt through a piece of muslin or a new all-purpose cloth over a bowl (secured with a rubber band). Transfer to the fridge and leave overnight for the yogurt to release its liquid and become firm and cheese-like. The next day, tip the strained yogurt into a clean bowl, add the garlic and cumin and season with salt and pepper. Chill in the fridge until ready to serve.

Preheat the oven to 190°C/Gas Mark 5. Warm the olive oil in a small saucepan, then add the ginger, cinnamon and chilli flakes.

Place the pumpkin in a roasting tin and baste with the warm oil. Add the red onion and season, then drizzle with the maple syrup and lemon juice. Bake for 15 minutes until the pumpkin is tender and starting to caramelize. Sprinkle with the sesame seasoning (or seeds) and set aside.

Combine all the dressing ingredients and whisk to emulsify.

When ready to serve, assemble the spinach and/or watercress, the herbs and tomatoes in a large bowl, then add the cooked quinoa and the dressing. Top with the pumpkin slices and sticky red onion, then add generous dollops of the garlicky labneh. Scatter with the walnuts and pumpkin seeds and serve.

See photograph on page 143.

Health Tip
Cumin really is our forever spice in the Midlife Kitchen, and not just for its fantastic aroma and taste; it contains a formidable array of bioactive compounds that can aid digestion and blood-sugar control.

WHY WE LOVE IT

These incredible veggie burgers were inspired by a visit to the Soul in a Bowl café in Sanur, one of those laid-back beachside places that have made Bali such a culinary hot spot. If you usually reach, in bored, bovine fashion, for meat when you think of burgers, our veggie version should convince you to ring the changes. Every ingredient has Midlife cred, from the lentils and squash, to the subtle spicing and the super-crisp coating of dukkah and red quinoa. You don't even need a bun – rest your burger instead on a bed of Little Gem lettuce and feel the bliss.

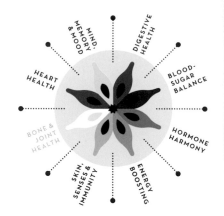

Bliss Burgers

WITH A RED QUINOA & DUKKAH CRUST

MAKES 4 BURGERS

250g butternut squash, peeled, deseeded and sliced

1 tsp olive oil

1 tsp cumin seeds

sea salt flakes and freshly ground black pepper

100g red lentils, rinsed

300ml water

1 bay leaf

200g firm tofu, cubed (optional)

2 spring onions, finely sliced

1 garlic clove, crushed

1 tsp Midlife Spice Mix, see page 24, or 1 tsp ground coriander and 1 tsp ground cumin

1 tsp chilli flakes

a handful of coriander (leaves and stalks), finely chopped

1 egg, beaten (if necessary)

light olive oil spray

FOR THE CRUST

2 tbsp uncooked red quinoa

2 tbsp Midlife Dukkah, see page 30, or 1 tbsp ground almonds and 2 tsp sesame seeds

TO SERVE

Little Gem lettuce leaves

Uchucuta, see page 226 (optional)

Health Tip
Butternut squash is chock-full of vitamin A, which plays an important role in maintaining the health of all body tissues, including skin, hair, teeth and bones.

Preheat the oven to 200°C/Gas Mark 6. Place the squash in a small roasting tin, drizzle with the olive oil, add the cumin seeds and season. Bake for 20–30 minutes until softened and beginning to colour at the edges. Leave to cool, then chop into small pieces.

Meanwhile, place the lentils, the water and bay leaf in a saucepan, bring to a simmer and cook for 10 minutes until tender but not overcooked. Remove the bay leaf, drain and leave to cool.

Place the cooled lentils, roasted butternut, tofu (if using), spring onions, garlic, spices and coriander in a large bowl and mix together. Season well, then divide the mixture into 4 and shape into burgers. If you find the mixture is too crumbly, add a beaten egg to bind.

Mix the crust ingredients in a shallow bowl. Coat each burger in the mixture, pressing gently. Chill in the fridge for at least 30 minutes.

Heat a large nonstick frying pan and spray with a little olive oil. Fry the burgers for 5–6 minutes on each side until golden and cooked through. Serve the burgers on Little Gem leaves, perhaps with Uchucuta on the side.

Midlife Hack: These are great eaten cold, making them ideal for packed lunches and picnics, so make a big batch to chill or freeze.

WHY WE LOVE IT

Gado gado, meaning 'medley' or 'mix', is a hugely popular Indonesian dish found on the menu at most street-side *warungs* (restaurants). The basis is just-cooked vegetables served with a chilli-hot peanut pouring sauce, but here we add shredded omelette, transforming it from a mere sideshow into a substantial (and beautiful) main event. You can use all or just a selection of the vegetables listed here.

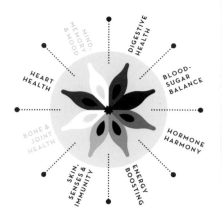

Gado Gado

WITH SHREDDED EGG

SERVES 2–3

FOR THE GADO GADO

1 large carrot, peeled and cut into thin batons

100g bean sprouts

100g trimmed green beans, cut into 3cm-long pieces

100g mangetout or sugar snap peas

100g baby sweetcorn, halved

1 small white cabbage, thinly sliced

1 head of pak choi, sliced

sea salt flakes

FOR THE PEANUT SAUCE

3 tbsp crunchy peanut butter (100% peanuts, no sugar)

2 tsp soy sauce

2 tsp soft brown sugar

1 garlic clove, finely chopped

a thumb-sized piece of fresh root ginger, peeled and grated

juice of 1 lime

1/2–1 tsp chilli flakes, to taste

75ml boiling water

FOR THE SHREDDED EGG

3 eggs

a splash of water

freshly ground black pepper

light olive oil spray

TO SERVE

2 spring onions, finely sliced

1 red chilli, deseeded and finely sliced

a handful of coriander leaves

a handful of unsalted peanuts

lime wedges

Health Tip
In recent studies, peanuts were found to be just as effective at helping to prevent heart disease as tree nuts – good news as they generally cost about half as much as premium nuts such as walnuts and almonds.

To make the peanut sauce, place all the ingredients, except the boiling water, in a bowl. Gradually add the water, slowly combining with a fork until everything is well mixed. The sauce should be runny enough to pour, so add more boiling water as necessary. Set aside.

Bring a large saucepan of salted water to the boil. Cook each vegetable in turn for a minute or so, then remove with a slotted spoon and drain on kitchen paper. Season with a little salt.

Whisk the eggs with a splash of water in a jug, then season with salt and pepper. Heat a large nonstick frying pan and spray with a little olive oil. Pour in half the egg mixture and roll it around to thinly cover the base of the pan. Cook for 1–2 minutes until lightly golden, then flip and cook on the other side. Remove from the pan and repeat with the remaining mixture to make a second omelette. Roll up the omelettes and slice across the rolls to form long, thin lengths.

Arrange the vegetables in a serving dish and drizzle with the peanut sauce. Drape with the shredded egg and top with the spring onions, chilli, coriander and peanuts. Any extra peanut sauce can be served on the side, along with the lime wedges.

WHY WE LOVE IT

There's something irresistible about the crunchy exterior and yielding centre of a good falafel – but the shop-bought versions often aren't that inspiring. There's no faff to making falafel at home: our version is quick and easy, using ingredients that can be grabbed in a rush from the kitchen cupboard. We've coated them in a few of our favourite things – dukkah, sesame seeds, LSA – for that all-important Midlife lift.

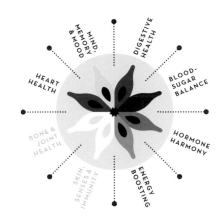

Fast Falafel

MAKES 8 SMALL OR 6 LARGE FALAFEL

FOR THE FALAFEL

400g can chickpeas, drained and rinsed

1 tbsp Midlife Spice Mix, see page 24, or 1 tsp ground coriander and 1 tsp ground cumin

1 egg

a large handful of flat leaf parsley

juice of 1/2 a lemon

sea salt flakes and freshly ground black pepper

1 tsp olive oil

FOR THE COATINGS

1 tbsp Midlife Sesame Seasoning, see page 32, or sesame seeds

or 1 tbsp Midlife Dukkah, see page 30

or 1 tbsp Midlife LSA, see page 27, or ground almonds

TO SERVE

2 wholemeal pitta breads

2 carrots, peeled and grated

2 tbsp hummus

2 tbsp Zehug, see page 238 (optional)

Place all the falafel ingredients, except the olive oil, in a food processor and blitz to a coarse paste. Shape the mixture into 8 small or 6 large patties. Coat each in your chosen coating, patting so it sticks well. They can be chilled at this point, and cooked later.

When ready to cook, heat the olive oil in a large frying pan, add the falafels and fry for 5–7 minutes on each side until golden brown on the outside and cooked through.

Serve in warm pittas, with the grated carrots, Zehug and hummus.

Try This...
Add any of the following to your falafel mix:

* 2 teaspoons grated lemon zest
* 1 teaspoon chilli flakes
* 1 teaspoon cumin seeds
* More chopped herbs, such as mint or coriander leaves
* Instead of Zehug and hummus, serve with: Beetroot Raita, see page 230; Wholly Guacamole, see page 220 or Roasted Red Pepper Hummus with Almonds & Paprika, see page 221

Health Tip
Chickpeas are a really affordable source of protein, slow-burn carbohydrates, minerals, vitamins, dietary fibre and health-promoting fatty acids... and you can make falafel with them!

WHY WE LOVE IT

A staple Ayurvedic healing food, this complete-protein meal nourishes and soothes the digestive system. It's essentially a Midlife take on kedgeree – traditionally made just with rice, but here we have added red lentils to improve the texture and boost the health credentials.

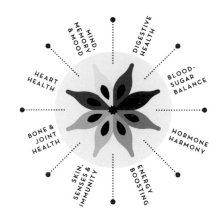

Red Lentil & Smoked Mackerel Kitchri

SERVES 2

1 tbsp olive oil or coconut oil

1 tsp mustard seeds

1 tsp nigella seeds

1 tbsp mild curry powder

2 tbsp Midlife Spice Mix, see page 24, or 3 tsp ground cumin, 2 tsp ground turmeric and 2 tsp ground coriander

1 small red onion, finely chopped

a splash of water

100g red lentils, rinsed

500ml vegetable stock

1 bay leaf

1 cinnamon stick, broken in 2

2 eggs

125g cooked basmati rice or ½ a pouch ready-cooked rice

150g smoked mackerel fillets, flaked

juice of ½ a lemon

sea salt flakes and freshly ground black pepper

coriander leaves, to serve

lemon wedges, to serve

Heat the oil in a large frying pan, add the mustard seeds and nigella seeds and fry for a couple of minutes, taking care not to burn them. Add the remaining ground spices and Spice Mix and fry for a further 30 seconds. Add the onion with a splash of water and fry gently for 2–3 minutes until softened.

Stir in the lentils and coat with the fragrant spice mixture, then add the stock, bay leaf and cinnamon stick. Bring to a simmer and cook for about 15 minutes until the lentils are tender.

Meanwhile, cook the eggs in a small saucepan of simmering water for 10 minutes until hard-boiled, then plunge into a bowl of cold water and leave to cool. Peel and quarter the eggs.

Stir the cooked rice into the lentils, then add the fish flakes and gently heat through. Add the lemon juice and season.

Spoon the kitchri into 2 bowls and top with the hard-boiled eggs. Scatter with coriander leaves, season with pepper and serve with lemon wedges.

Health Tip
Substituting mackerel for the more conventional haddock increases the omega-3 fatty acid content in this dish – great for your heart and joints.

WHY WE LOVE IT

We're forever on the hunt for speedy suppers that are just a bit special – and this fits the bill perfectly. It's one of those dishes that tastes as though it's been hours in the making, but in fact the prep couldn't be easier, and most of the ingredients (bar the fish) are probably already lurking in your fridge. Simply add a sturdy white fish – we've used monkfish here, but halibut would be equally delicious – or calamari and king prawns, and eat with a warm wholemeal pitta to mop up the densely savoury juices. Very little could improve it, but Sam says a glass of chilled Sancerre works a treat.

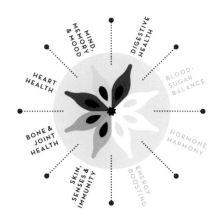

Monkfish & Fennel

WITH HERBS, TOMATOES & ANCHOVIES

SERVES 2

2 tsp olive oil

½ a fennel bulb, trimmed and thinly sliced

4 ripe tomatoes, quartered

4 anchovy fillets, chopped

sea salt and freshly ground black pepper

250g monkfish fillet or tail, membrane removed and cut into 3cm-thick medallions

a handful of Greek olives, pitted and chopped

a handful of coriander leaves, chopped

a handful of basil leaves

a handful of dill, chopped

Heat the olive oil in a medium frying pan, add the fennel and sauté for several minutes until softened, then add the tomatoes and anchovies. Season and simmer for 10–15 minutes until the tomatoes start to soften (see Midlife Hack).

Add the monkfish medallions and olives, cover with a lid and simmer for a further 5–10 minutes until the fish is cooked through. Stir through the herbs and serve.

Midlife Hack: You can cook the recipe to this point, then cool and refrigerate until required.

Health Tip
Every ingredient in this dish is a Midlife winner, but the real superstar is fennel. Its phytonutrients help maintain healthy bones, decrease blood pressure and promote heart and gut health. It can even help boost the elasticity of your skin.

WHY WE LOVE IT

This zingy green sauce pays homage to the fabulous flavours of Thailand and is the perfect partner for a piece of oily fish. Our favourite is a pale-pink and delicate trout fillet, flash-fried to give it a crisp skin, but the dressing would work well with any fish fillet: salmon, snapper, sea bass or sea bream would all be excellent. For maximum Midlife points, try it with fresh grilled mackerel or sardines.

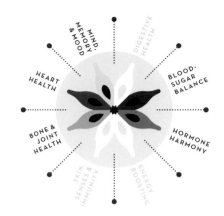

MIND, MEMORY & MOOD

DIGESTIVE HEALTH

HEART HEALTH

BLOOD-SUGAR BALANCE

BONE & JOINT HEALTH

HORMONE HARMONY

SKIN, SENSES & IMMUNITY

ENERGY BOOSTING

Crispy Trout
WITH ASIAN SALSA

SERVES 2

2 trout fillets, about 125g each, with skin on

a little olive oil

sea salt flakes and freshly ground black pepper

coriander leaves, to serve

FOR THE SALSA

a handful of coriander (leaves and stalks), roughly chopped

a thumb-sized piece of fresh root ginger, peeled and chopped

a thumb-sized piece of fresh turmeric, peeled and chopped

1 garlic clove, peeled and halved

2 spring onions, roughly chopped

1 large red chilli, deseeded and roughly chopped, or to taste

juice of 1 lime

2 tsp sesame oil

2 tsp soy sauce

2 tsp runny honey

1 tsp Thai fish sauce (nam pla)

Place all the salsa ingredients in a food processor and pulse to form a coarse paste.

Heat a griddle pan or large frying pan over a high heat until it is hot enough to crisp the trout skin. Drizzle the fish with a little olive oil and season well, then place, skin-side down, in the hot pan, pressing lightly. Cook for 3–4 minutes until the skin turns crisp. Gently flip the fillets, reduce the heat and cook for a further 2–3 minutes until the fish is cooked through and opaque (the timing will depend on the thickness of the fish).

Serve immediately, drizzled with a good amount of the zingy salsa.

Health Tip
There is an ever-increasing body of evidence to suggest that regular consumption of fish, and in particular oily fish like trout, reduces the risk of cardiovascular disease. They're also a good source of vitamin D, the 'sunshine vitamin', which benefits the bones and immune system.

WHY WE LOVE IT

Ginger is a staple ingredient in the Midlife Kitchen, and here we use the pickled version more commonly found sitting alongside sushi and wasabi. We adore its delicate flavour and elegant ballerina-pink colour, an unexpected complement to the clean crunch of sugar snaps in this quick, bright dish. We've used king prawns here, but chicken would work well for a great low-cal, high-flavour lunch.

Miso King Prawns

WITH SESAME & PICKLED GINGER SUGAR SNAPS

SERVES 2

8 large raw peeled king prawns

1 tsp coconut oil

2 tbsp rice vinegar or mirin

FOR THE MARINADE

2 tbsp brown miso paste

2 tbsp soy sauce

2 tsp sesame oil

2cm piece of fresh root ginger, peeled and finely grated

juice of 1 lime

FOR THE SALAD

100g sugar snap peas

100g mangetout

sea salt flakes

2 tbsp pickled ginger, from a jar

2 tbsp sesame seeds

Combine all the marinade ingredients in a bowl and add the prawns. Cover with clingfilm and leave to marinate in the fridge for at least 10 minutes, or several hours if you have time.

Cook the sugar snaps and mangetout in a saucepan of salted boiling water for 2 minutes until just tender. Drain and refresh in very cold water (this will help retain their colour and crunch). Drain well and pat dry with kitchen paper, then slice on the diagonal and transfer to a bowl. Combine with the pickled ginger and sesame seeds.

Heat a griddle pan until hot, add the coconut oil and prawns, including the marinade, and fry for 1 minute or so on each side until they turn pink and are cooked through. Remove the prawns from the pan and keep warm. Add the rice vinegar or mirin to the pan, stirring in any sticky bits from the base of the pan.

Serve the prawns with the pretty salad and drizzled with the pan juices.

Health Tip
Astaxanthin, a pinkish-orange pigment found in many marine foods (prawns, crab and salmon), has powerful antioxidant and cardio-protective properties.

WHY WE LOVE IT

A simple piece of fish is a glorious thing – low in calories, high in protein – and it's better still when given the Midlife treatment with this collection of antioxidant super spices. Here, we've paired haddock loin with 'sabji', an Indian-style vegetable stir-fry. We've chosen asparagus for our sabji – a glorious addition to the Midlife menu thanks to its anti-inflammatory saponins, gut-friendly prebiotic inulin and B-vits, which help with blood-sugar management. Cook the asparagus quickly in lemon and spice, keeping it deliciously *al dente*, with the petits pois adding sweetness.

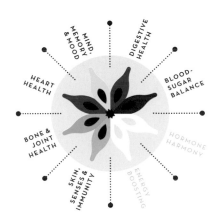

MIND, MEMORY & MOOD

DIGESTIVE HEALTH

HEART HEALTH

BLOOD-SUGAR BALANCE

BONE & JOINT HEALTH

HORMONE HARMONY

SKIN, SENSES & IMMUNITY

ENERGY BOOSTING

Indian Spiced Fish

WITH ASPARAGUS & PEA SABJI

SERVES 2

2 tsp ground cumin

1 tsp hot curry powder

1/2 tsp ground cinnamon

1/2 tsp ground turmeric

sea salt and freshly ground black pepper

2 tbsp vegetable oil

2 skinless loins of white fish (haddock, cod, hake or pollock), about 125g each

FOR THE SABJI

light olive oil spray

1/2 tsp coriander seeds

1/2 tsp fennel seeds

250g fine asparagus, trimmed and cut into 4cm-long pieces

60ml water

juice of 1/2 a lemon

1 tsp peeled and finely grated fresh root ginger

sea salt and freshly ground black pepper

100g frozen petits pois

FOR THE YOGURT TOPPING

4 tbsp natural yogurt

a handful of mint leaves, thinly sliced

Place the cumin, curry powder, cinnamon and turmeric in a small bowl with a pinch of salt and a grind of black pepper. Add the vegetable oil to make a paste.

Marinate the fish in the spice paste for at least 15 minutes in the fridge, to allow the flavours to develop.

Preheat the oven to 180°C/Gas Mark 4. Place the marinated fish in a foil-lined baking tray and bake for 15–20 minutes until the fish is cooked through and flakes easily.

Meanwhile, make the sabji. Heat a nonstick frying pan and spray with olive oil. Add the coriander and fennel seeds and when they start to pop, add the asparagus and fry for 1 minute, then add the water, lemon juice and ginger.

Season and simmer for 2 minutes, then add the peas and cook for a further 2 minutes until most of the liquid has evaporated and the vegetables are just cooked.

Combine the yogurt and mint in a small bowl.

To assemble the dish, transfer the sabji to a serving plate, top with the fish and the minty yogurt.

Health Tip
Common or garden peas improve gastrointestinal function and reduce glycaemic load, which basically means they can help keep your digestion on track and your blood-sugar levels steady.

WHY WE LOVE IT

This peppy mustard marinade brings a whole new angle to any white fish – almost as if it's dressed in the perfect condiments from the get-go. Halibut, a delicate oily fish that is simplicity itself to cook, makes a great heart-healthy alternative to the usual cod fillets, though this marinade and method would work equally well with any fish or meat.

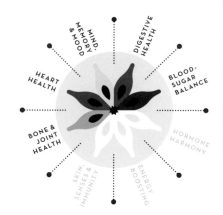

Grilled Mustard & Herb Halibut

SERVES 2

2 shallots, roughly chopped

2 garlic cloves, peeled and halved

2 tbsp Dijon mustard

2 tsp dried Herbes de Provence

a squeeze of lemon juice

1 tsp apple cider vinegar

1 tsp mustard seeds

sea salt flakes and freshly ground black pepper

2 halibut fillets, 150–200g each, skin removed

watercress salad, to serve (optional)

Put the shallots, garlic, mustard, herbs, a squeeze of lemon juice and apple cider vinegar in a food processor and whizz to produce a smooth paste, making sure the shallots have been well blitzed so that they cook quickly under the grill. Stir in the mustard seeds and season.

Place the fish in a dish and coat with the paste. Cover with clingfilm and leave to marinate in the fridge for at least 30 minutes, or preferably overnight to ensure a good depth of flavour.

Transfer the marinated fish to a foil-lined baking tray and cook under a preheated hot grill for 3–5 minutes on each side until the fish is cooked through and flakes easily (the timing will depend on the thickness of the fish).

Serve immediately, perhaps with a simple watercress salad.

Midlife Hack: Quickly peel shallots by placing them in a bowl of boiling water for 5 minutes first to help release the skins. Let them cool a bit before you embark!

Health Tip
Halibut is a lovely firm-fleshed white fish that is a good source of protein, as well as providing omega-3s, B vits and essential minerals phosphorus and selenium – great for energy and for keeping bones and joints strong.

WHY WE LOVE IT

These are definitely a bit swish, but the name comes from our Swedish spin on a Swiss classic, the much-loved rösti. Our Midlife makeover uses gravadlax, a Nordic smoked salmon packed with omega-3s, and replaces half the regular potato with sweet potato to increase the vitamin A content; retaining the potato skins will increase the amount of fibre in your rösti and help with the all-important crunch.

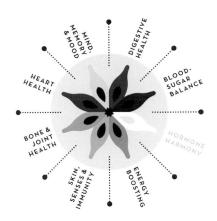

Swish Rösti

WITH GRAVADLAX & DILL YOGURT

MAKES 6–8 RÖSTI

250g white potatoes, scrubbed and cut into large pieces

250g sweet potatoes, scrubbed and cut into large pieces

sea salt flakes

150g gravadlax slices

2 spring onions, finely sliced

freshly ground black pepper

2 tsp olive oil

1 tsp butter

green salad, to serve (optional)

lemon wedges, to serve

FOR THE DILL YOGURT

4 tbsp natural yogurt

juice of ½ a lemon

a handful of dill, finely chopped

Health Tip

Both regular potatoes and sweet potatoes deserve a place in your diet, but orange sweet potatoes are vitamin A superstars; they also tend to be higher in potentially helpful phytochemicals, such as the antioxidant defensin.

Cook the potatoes and sweet potatoes in a large saucepan of salted boiling water for 10 minutes until they are starting to soften but not cooked through. Drain, then leave to cool. Place in the fridge and chill for a few hours or overnight (or place in the freezer for 15 minutes).

When chilled, grate the potatoes using the coarse side of a grater. Cut 100g of the gravadlax into ribbons.

Using your fingers, combine the grated potato, gravadlax ribbons, spring onions and salt and pepper in a large bowl until everything is well mixed. Take handfuls of the mixture and shape into 6–8 palm-sized rösti. Aim for thin patties, squeezing to compress them into shape.

Heat the olive oil and butter in a large frying pan, add the rösti, about 4 at time depending on the size of your pan. Cook over a medium heat for about 10 minutes on each side – press down with a spatula to flatten and ensure they are crisp and golden brown. Remove from the pan and repeat with the remaining rösti mixture.

Meanwhile, combine the dill yogurt ingredients in a bowl.

When cooked, place the rösti on a large plate and top with the remaining slices of gravadlax. Serve with the dill yogurt, a green salad and lemon wedges on the side.

WHY WE LOVE IT

The tuna and bean salad is an all-time classic – a harmonious marriage of healthy ingredients that just happen to be lurking in the larder. Tuscans are sometimes referred to as *mangiafagioli* or 'bean eaters', and the prevalence of beans in their cooking is one of the reasons that an Italian diet is considered so healthy. Beans are primed with good things: protein, fibre, vats of vits, while the tuna and red onion of the classic dish bring bold flavour to the gathering.

MIND, MEMORY & MOOD

DIGESTIVE HEALTH

HEART HEALTH

BLOOD-SUGAR BALANCE

BONE & JOINT HEALTH

HORMONE HARMONY

SKIN, SENSES & IMMUNITY

ENERGY BOOSTING

Classic Tuna Fagioli

SERVES 2

2 x 200g cans different beans, such as kidney, haricot, cannellini or butter beans, or a 400g can mixed beans, drained and rinsed

½ a small red onion, thinly sliced

160g can tuna in olive oil, drained

a handful of parsley, chopped, plus extra to serve

4 tbsp Midlife Salad Dressing, see page 33

finely sliced lemon zest, to serve

Place the beans, onion, tuna and parsley in a bowl. Add the dressing, mix well and chill for at least 30 minutes in the fridge to allow the flavours to mingle and develop.

Serve sprinkled with lemon zest and chopped parsley.

WHY WE LOVE IT

Given this is such a standard, we've created an alternative version starring peppered smoked mackerel, fennel and dill to take your fagioli fork in a whole new direction. The extra virgin olive oil in the Midlife Dressing is crucial here – you'll want the tang of a really good, grass-green oil; you also need plenty of lemon juice and zest to add a note of acidity (and more antioxidant goodness).

Midlife Mackerel Fagioli

WITH FENNEL & DILL

SERVES 2

2 x 200g cans different beans, such as kidney, haricot, cannellini or butter beans or a 400g can mixed beans, drained and rinsed

½ a small red onion, thinly sliced

150g peppered smoked mackerel fillets, skin removed, torn into bite-sized pieces

½ a small fennel bulb, trimmed and thinly sliced

a handful of dill, plus extra to serve

4 tbsp Midlife Salad Dressing, see page 33

finely sliced lemon zest, to serve

Place the beans, onion, mackerel, fennel and dill in a bowl. Add the dressing, mix well and chill for at least 30 minutes in the fridge to allow the flavours to mingle and develop.

Serve sprinkled with lemon zest and chopped dill.

Health Tip
A 2009 study found that daily consumption of onions improves bone density in menopausal women, reducing the risk of hip fractures.

WHY WE LOVE IT

Think of this aromatic bowlful as moules marinière meets tom yum soup. It's incredibly simple and ready in minutes, which belies its sophisticated appearance, making for a pretty impressive dinner-party starter or light lunch.

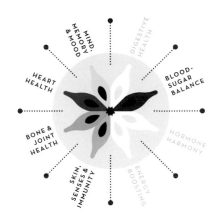

Thai Midlife Mussels

SERVES 2

1kg fresh mussels

1 tsp coconut oil

a thumb-sized piece of fresh root ginger, peeled and finely grated

a thumb-sized piece of fresh turmeric root, peeled and finely chopped

4 shallots, thinly sliced

2 garlic cloves, crushed

1 lemon grass stalk, tough outer layers removed, finely minced

1 large red chilli, deseeded and finely chopped, or to taste

500ml fish or vegetable stock

1 tsp runny honey

1 tbsp Thai fish sauce (nam pla)

juice of 1 lime

a small handful of coriander leaves, chopped

a small handful of mint leaves, chopped

Rinse and scrub the mussels thoroughly, removing the beards and discarding any that are cracked or aren't tightly shut.

Heat the coconut oil in a wide saucepan or wok, add the ginger, turmeric, shallots, garlic, lemon grass and chilli and fry gently for about 3 minutes until softened. Add the stock, honey and fish sauce and bring to a simmer.

Add the mussels, cover with a lid and cook for 5 minutes, or until all the mussels have opened. Discard any that remain closed.

Stir in the lime juice and herbs and it's ready to eat.

Midlife Hack: If you crave carbs, or want a more filling meal, this works really well with cooked brown rice added to the bowl once you've eaten the mussels, to soak up the lovely golden broth.

Health Tip
Mussels have an impressive nutritional profile, containing long-chain fatty acids that can improve brain function and help reduce inflammatory conditions such as arthritis.

WHY WE LOVE IT

This is a light, fragrant curry, alive with the flavours of Southeast Asia. Using our Midlife Curry Paste speeds up the process considerably, so, apart from the time it takes for the chicken to cook through, it requires no more than 15 minutes effort on your part to produce something pretty spectacular.

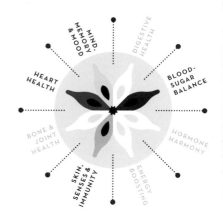

Balinese Yellow Chicken Curry

SERVES 4

1 tbsp coconut oil

5 tbsp Midlife Curry Paste, see page 34

2 lemon grass stalks, bashed with a rolling pin

4 kaffir lime leaves, crushed

2 tsp tamarind paste

1kg boneless chicken thighs and drumsticks, skin removed

350ml chicken stock

400ml can coconut milk

juice of 2 limes

a large handful of coriander leaves, left whole, to serve

sea salt flakes and ground white pepper

Heat the coconut oil in a large wok or deep saucepan, add the curry paste and fry over a high heat for about 1 minute until fragrant. Reduce the heat, add the lemon grass, lime leaves and tamarind paste and cook, stirring, for a further minute.

Add the chicken and cook for a couple of minutes on each side to get a little colour, then add the stock. Bring to the boil, then reduce the heat, cover with a lid and simmer gently for 40 minutes, or until the chicken is cooked through.

Add the coconut milk and lime juice and simmer for a further 5 minutes. Season and scatter with the coriander leaves, then serve. Brown or red rice is an excellent partner for this dish and, as with most curries, it tastes even better reheated the next day.

Midlife Hack: Keep any leftover coconut milk in the fridge to stir into your morning porridge with chopped banana, a pinch of salt and a dash of date syrup.

Health Tip
Tamarind is a tangy, pulpy fruit that tastes like apricots, dates and lemons combined – giving a sweet/ sour hit to many South Asian dishes. It provides iron and magnesium, important for maintaining healthy muscles, including the heart.

WHY WE LOVE IT

This is one-pot Midlife cooking at its best: lots of lean protein, plenty of slow-burn carbs, bags of herby flavour and a solitary pan to wash up at the end. Make this your new Sunday roast and you'll be able to stick it in the oven, play a game of tennis or tiddlywinks and return to a complete family meal. Job done.

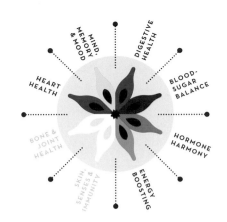

Pot-roast Chicken

WITH LENTILS, PARSLEY, SAGE, ROSEMARY & THYME

SERVES 4

1 tbsp vegetable oil

2 onions, diced

4 garlic cloves, peeled and halved

2 rosemary sprigs, leaves picked and chopped

225g red lentils, rinsed

a handful of thyme sprigs, tied with string

5 sage leaves

750ml chicken stock, plus extra if needed

juice of 1 lemon (retain the squeezed lemon halves)

1 medium free-range chicken, about 1.5–1.8kg

2 tsp butter, softened

sea salt flakes and freshly ground black pepper

a handful of flat leaf parsley, chopped

Preheat the oven to 180°C/Gas Mark 4.

Heat the oil in a large casserole dish, add the onions and cook over a medium heat for a few minutes until softened. Add the garlic and rosemary and cook for a further 3 minutes, then stir in the lentils, thyme, sage leaves and stock. Stir in the lemon juice and add the squeezed lemon husks.

Smear the chicken with the butter and season well. Nestle it into the lentil mix and bring to a simmer, then transfer to the oven. Bake, uncovered, for 1 hour 15 minutes until the chicken is golden brown and the juices run clear when the thickest part of the thigh is pierced with a knife. Check occasionally that the lentils aren't too dry (if they are, add a little more stock or boiling water and give it a stir). Remove the chicken from the casserole and leave to rest.

Check the lentils for seasoning, remove the lemon husks, stir in the sticky bits from the side of the dish and add plenty of chopped parsley. Carve the chicken and serve with the lentils.

Midlife Hack: If you crave leafy greens with this, try some oven-baked kale. Empty a bag of sliced kale into a roasting tin, toss in a teaspoon or two of olive oil and a scatter of sea salt flakes, then pop in the oven about 15 minutes before the chicken comes out.

Health Tip
Herbs are a wonderful way to add multi-layered flavour without resorting to salt, sugar or fat. What's more, the vitamins and antioxidants in these Scarborough Fair herbs can benefit midlifers on many levels, including giving a boost to cognitive function.

WHY WE LOVE IT

If you're feeding a gang, nothing beats a slow-roasted joint – the kind of meal you can prep quickly in advance, whack in a low oven and forget until the aromas entice you back to the kitchen for the final hurrah. It's a great Italian and Middle Eastern tradition, based on the provocative principle that slow-cooked meat becomes gorgeously tender, requiring little more than a tug to carve. This is our Midlife version, packed with our favourite garlic and Midlife Spice Mix. A roasted fig on the side simply adds another divine dimension to something that is already heavenly.

Slow-roasted Lamb
WITH STICKY FIGS

SERVES 8

1 large leg of lamb (on the bone), about 2.5kg

juice of 1 lemon

FOR THE PASTE

75g butter, softened

4 tbsp Midlife Spice Mix, see page 24

1 tbsp cumin seeds

1 tsp chilli flakes

1 tsp ground turmeric

2 tsp dried mixed herbs

5 garlic cloves, crushed

1 tbsp sea salt flakes

freshly ground black pepper

FOR THE FIGS

12–16 ripe fresh figs, scored with a cross

1 tbsp pomegranate molasses

1 tbsp extra virgin olive oil

sea salt flakes and freshly ground black pepper

Health Tip
Figs contain prebiotics, a type of fibre that passes through the gut undigested and stimulates the growth of 'good' bacteria, improving digestive health.

Preheat the oven to 150°C/Gas Mark 2. Score the lamb deeply with a sharp knife and place it in a large roasting tin. Combine all the paste ingredients in a bowl to make a spicy, herby garlic butter. Rub the paste into the lamb, pressing well into the incisions.

Roast for 4–5 hours (it will depend on the lamb, and even on the season), basting every so often to keep it moist, until the meat is dark golden and sticky. Remove from the oven, leaving the oven on, and place on a platter, cover loosely in foil and leave to rest for up to 30 minutes.

About 10 minutes before serving, turn the oven up to 200°C/Gas Mark 6. Place the figs in a small baking tin, drizzle with the pomegranate molasses and olive oil, then season. Bake for 10 minutes until just softened and blistered.

Meanwhile, remove the excess oil from the lamb roasting tin, leaving the sticky deposits. Place the tin on the hob and add the lemon juice. Stir well over a medium heat to release the caramelized, almost burnt bits from the base of the tin, adding a little water if it needs more liquid (you're looking for a few tablespoons of reduction, not a gravy).

Serve the warm lamb with the juices, and the roasted figs hot from the oven. A green salad with pomegranate seeds is a good accompaniment.

WHY WE LOVE IT

Another of our Midlife observations is that our appetite for red meat has declined dramatically – so this main meal gives spiced veg the starring role. What you get is a sticky bed of sweet veggie goodness, with the slender slivers of seared steak introduced as a decadent garnish. On a more prosaic note, it's a cheap way to make a steak go around.

Seared Sirloin on Pan-roasted Veg

WITH A SPICED BALSAMIC GLAZE

SERVES 4

300g sirloin steak, about 2.5cm thick

sea salt flakes and freshly ground black pepper

1 tsp vegetable oil

FOR THE GLAZED VEG

1 tbsp olive oil

2 tsp nigella seeds

2 tsp mustard seeds

2 tsp coriander seeds

3 small peppers (red, orange and yellow), deseeded and cut into chunks

1 courgette, cut into 2cm chunks

1 small aubergine, cut into 2cm chunks

4 shallots, peeled and halved

4 garlic cloves, crushed

1 red chilli, deseeded and finely sliced, or to taste

a handful of oregano leaves (or herbs of your choice)

juice of 1 lemon

1 tbsp balsamic vinegar

125g baby spinach leaves

Preheat the oven to 180°C/Gas Mark 4.

First prepare the glazed veg. Heat the olive oil in a small frying pan, add the seeds and fry for several minutes until they start to colour and pop, taking care not to burn them.

Place the veggies, shallots, garlic and chilli in a large roasting tin, dress with the warm spiced oil, then add the oregano, lemon juice and balsamic vinegar. Bake for 30 minutes until the veg are softened and lightly charred. Add the spinach to the tray, return to the oven and bake for a further 5 minutes until wilted.

Meanwhile, generously season the steak with salt and pepper. Heat the vegetable oil in a small frying pan, add the steak and fry until cooked to your liking: 1 1/2 minutes on each side for rare; 3 minutes on each side for medium; 4 minutes on each side for well done. Leave to rest for at least 5 minutes, then thinly slice.

Divide the baked veggies among 4 bowls, then top with the steak and serve.

Health Tip
Red meat is, of course, a great source of iron, which is important for preventing anaemia and boosting energy. The iron found in meat is called haem iron, more easily absorbed by the body than the iron found in plants.

WHY WE LOVE IT

One of the joys of writing a cookbook is that you get to eat *a lot* of food, often several times in one sitting, just to finesse a recipe. So it was that we found ourselves tucking into these kick-ass pork chops at 8.30 one morning. We finished the lot, and then popped a few more under the grill, just to *make sure* – a bit like Pooh with his honey pots. Meat doesn't feature heavily in the Midlife Kitchen, so when you do eat it, try to buy the best you can and treat it like a king: give it gorgeous accessories and allow it to rest well before it hits the plate.

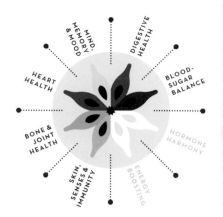

Uchucuta Pork

SERVES 4

4 thick pork chops, about 250g each, trimmed

1 quantity (approx. 8 tbsp) Uchucuta, see page 226, plus extra to serve (optional)

Marinate the chops in the Uchucuta for a couple of hours or overnight in the fridge.

Place the chops, doused in plenty of the sauce, on a foil-lined baking tray. Cook under a preheated hot grill for 4–5 minutes on each side until the meat is cooked through and the fat is gently charred. Remove from the heat and leave to rest for 5 minutes.

Serve the chops with the juices from the foil and a spoonful of extra Uchucuta on the side (don't use any uncooked sauce that has been in contact with the raw meat).

These chops would sit very nicely alongside our Zesty Tenderstem with Midlife Dukkah & Chilli, see page 193.

Midlife Hack: These chops also cook brilliantly on a barbecue; try an Uchucuta marinade with pork loin (really slather it on and roast quickly) or with lamb chops, rack of lamb or chicken wings.

Health Tip
Lean protein is essential for muscle growth and maintenance. After the age of 30, we lose up to 8 per cent of our muscle mass each decade, so include protein – such as lean pork, chicken, fish, eggs or legumes – in your daily diet to stave off decline.

WHY WE LOVE IT

These are essentially thin omelettes laced with spinach, which serve as a great green wrap to be filled with whatever takes your fancy. Here we keep it simple with tomato and avocado, but it works just as well with sautéed vegetables, crumbled cheese, smoked salmon, caramelized onions, guacamole and jalapeños – you name it. They are a brilliantly versatile alternative to bread or wheat wraps for lunch and it goes without saying that they make a superb breakfast.

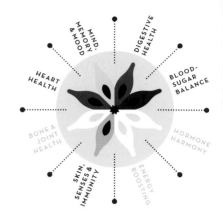

Green Egg Wraps

MAKES 2

2 large eggs

a splash of water

sea salt flakes and freshly ground black pepper

light olive oil spray

a large handful of spinach leaves

FOR THE FILLING

1 ripe tomato, diced

1 small ripe avocado, peeled, stoned and chopped

1 spring onion, finely sliced

a squeeze of lemon juice

1 tbsp Midlife Spiced Seed Mix, see page 26, to serve (optional)

Place the eggs in a bowl, add a splash of water and whisk together, then season with salt and pepper.

Heat a medium nonstick frying pan and spray with a little olive oil. Add a small handful of the spinach (just a few leaves in a single layer in the pan) and cook for about 20 seconds until just starting to wilt. Pour in half the egg mixture and roll it around to thinly cover the base of the pan. Cook until golden (it will take no more than a minute), then flip and cook on the other side. Remove from the pan and set aside. Repeat with the remaining egg mixture and spinach to make a second wrap.

Fill the wraps with the tomato, avocado and spring onion, adding a squeeze of lemon juice to give some acidity. Roll up the wraps, top with the spiced seeds and serve.

Health Tip
When buying spinach, the greener the better – it indicates higher levels of health-giving carotenoids, which are important for eye health, guarding against macular degeneration, a leading cause of vision loss in the over 50s.

WHY WE LOVE IT

This is a brilliant, brilliant little lunch idea. Brilliant because we use seaweed as a healthy alternative to a traditional wheat wrap – the nori provides fibre, iron, calcium and other essential minerals, so it's an excellent choice to help protect your heart and bones – and brilliant again because it uses up any leftovers you may have in the fridge. Surplus rice, quinoa, cooked chicken, prawns and salad all come together in Japan-easy, sushi-style rolls, thanks to the yummy sesame soy dressing.

Asian Salad Nori Wraps

SERVES 2

a small handful of coriander leaves, chopped

1 small carrot, peeled and very finely sliced

1/2 a cucumber, deseeded and very finely sliced

1 small Little Gem lettuce, finely sliced

2 spring onions, finely sliced on the diagonal

100g cooked chicken or prawns or firm tofu (optional)

2 tbsp Miso, Sesame & Ginger Dressing, see page 119, plus extra to serve

1 tsp Midlife Sesame Seasoning, see page 32, or sesame seeds

4 dried nori seaweed sheets (the kind used for sushi)

250g cooked rice or quinoa, or a ready-cooked pouch of either

Place the coriander, vegetables and your choice of chicken, prawns or tofu in a bowl and combine. Add the dressing, sprinkle with the sesame seasoning or seeds and toss well.

Lay a nori seaweed sheet on a chopping board, add a thin layer of cooked rice or quinoa, leaving a strip at the end to seal the wrap. Layer a small handful of the vegetable mix over the rice and roll up as tightly as you can without tearing the nori sheet. Moisten the edge with a little water or dressing and finish rolling to create a cigar shape. Repeat with the remaining ingredients to form 4 wraps.

Cut the wraps in half diagonally and serve with extra dressing as a dipping sauce.

Health Tip
Sesame seeds are a good source of fibre, B vits and magnesium, which can help to keep blood pressure healthy.

WHY WE LOVE IT

We've yet to meet anyone who doesn't adore rice paper wraps, but we tend to eat them on the rare occasions we go to a Vietnamese restaurant – which is a shame, because they're so easy to make at home. You can use whatever you like as a filling, but our absolute favourite is this crab and avocado duo, served with an authentic sweet-and-sour dipping sauce.

Vietnamese Crabocado Wraps

WITH SWEET & SOUR DIPPING SAUCE

MAKES 8

8 rice paper roll wrappers

1 large carrot, peeled and very finely sliced

1/2 a cucumber, deseeded and very finely sliced

3 spring onions, very finely sliced

FOR THE FILLING

100g fresh white crabmeat

finely grated zest and juice of 1 lime

1 tbsp natural yogurt

1/2 a ripe avocado, peeled and sliced

a handful of coriander leaves, chopped

a handful of mint leaves, chopped

sea salt flakes and freshly ground black pepper

FOR THE DIPPING SAUCE

juice of 2 limes

2 tsp runny honey

2 tbsp Thai fish sauce (nam pla)

2 tbsp rice vinegar

1 tbsp finely chopped coriander leaves

1 garlic clove, crushed

1 large red chilli, deseeded and very finely chopped

Combine all the filling ingredients in a bowl, then cover with clingfilm and chill in the fridge.

Mix all the dipping sauce ingredients in a separate bowl, stirring well. Set aside.

Lay a rice paper wrapper on a chopping board. Using a pastry brush, moisten the sheet lightly with warm water so that it softens. Place a few lengths of carrot, cucumber and spring onion horizontally at the top of the wrapper, then spread 1 heaped tablespoon of the filling in a line beneath the veggies, so that a third of the rice paper is covered.

Take the top edge of the wrapper and fold it down over the filling. Fold the edges in from the left and right and keep rolling, tucking in the edges as you go, as if you are wrapping a present. It's a little fiddly, but aim to create a fairly tight cylinder – the rice paper is quite elastic when wet so it can be stretched and manhandled fairly easily. Repeat with the remaining ingredients to make 8 wraps.

Serve with the dipping sauce on the side.

Health Tip
Crabmeat is crammed with essential nutrients including protein, healthy fats, B vits and important minerals such as zinc, selenium and iodine; it contains phosphorus, too, which, alongside calcium, is important for strong bones.

SIDES
&
SNACKS

WHY WE LOVE IT

Spinach is the original power veg, the ninja of the salad drawer, loaded with nutrients in a glorious low-calorie package. Its health credentials are in no doubt, so it's great to find some new weekday ways to prepare it. A comforting combo of spinach, onion and mushrooms is given a twist with dill, and stirred through with yogurt for a silky finish. Though great as a side dish, this would also be gorgeous on toasted seedy bread, crowned with a poached egg.

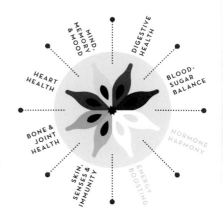

Wilted Spinach

WITH SAUTÉED MUSHROOMS & DILL

SERVES 2

250g spinach leaves

2 tbsp water

1 tsp extra virgin olive oil or butter

1 small red onion, finely diced

1 garlic clove, crushed

250g chestnut mushrooms, sliced

a handful of dill, roughly chopped

sea salt flakes and freshly ground black pepper

2 tbsp natural yogurt

1 tbsp lemon juice

½ tsp paprika

Place the spinach in a large frying pan over a medium heat, add the water and cook for 2–3 minutes until wilted. Transfer to a sieve and press with the back of a spoon to remove any moisture, then pat dry with kitchen paper and roughly chop.

Heat the olive oil or butter in a small frying pan, add the onion and garlic and fry gently for about 3 minutes until softened. Add the mushrooms and fry for 3 minutes, then stir in the chopped spinach and dill and cook for a further 3 minutes. Season as necessary.

Combine the yogurt, lemon juice and paprika in a small bowl, then swirl into the spinach mix, heat through and serve.

Health Tip
There is encouraging research showing that foods rich in vitamin A, such as spinach, may have a modest protective effect against breast cancer. This is just one of the many good reasons to eat plenty of spinach in midlife.

WHY WE LOVE IT

This is a great dish to make in advance as the flavours develop when given a little time to sit and get to know each other. Puy lentils are a very fine thing indeed – nutty, punchy, protein-packed and unbelievably easy to prepare – particularly if, like us, you use a ready-cooked pouch.

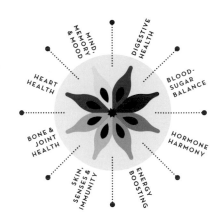

Puy Lentils
WITH FETA & ROASTED TOMATOES

SERVES 4

250g pouch ready-cooked Puy lentils, or 200g dried Puy lentils plus 1 litre water

sea salt flakes and freshly ground black pepper

20 cherry tomatoes on the vine

1 tsp olive oil

1 tbsp apple cider vinegar

1 garlic clove, finely chopped

1 small red onion, finely diced

1 tsp runny honey

1 tbsp extra virgin olive oil

60g feta cheese, crumbled

1 tbsp lemon juice

a handful of mint leaves, chopped

If using dried lentils, place them in a pan with 1 litre of water, bring to the boil, then reduce the heat and simmer until tender. Drain, season with a little salt and pepper and set aside to cool.

Preheat the oven to 170°C/Gas Mark 3½.

Place the tomatoes in a small baking tin, drizzle with the olive oil and season with salt and pepper. Bake for 10–15 minutes until blistered and soft.

Meanwhile, put the remaining ingredients into a serving bowl with the lentils and mix well. Add the roasted tomatoes and juices from the tin, stir through and it's ready to serve.

Health Tip
Eat more lentils! Not only are they packed with beneficial fibre, protein, minerals and vitamins, they are also low in calories and contain virtually no fat. And they taste great too.

WHY WE LOVE IT

Here's a fresh and fragrant Balinese staple that's usually served as one of the components of 'nasi campur', a pick-and-mix of rice, meat, salads and sambals. Urab is a simple but incredibly tasty combination of green beans and fresh coconut, with a chilli kick coming from our Midlife Curry Paste. If you're a bit bored with green beans, this will give them a whole new lease of life.

Urab

BALINESE GREEN BEAN & COCONUT SALAD

SERVES 4

300g fine green beans, trimmed and halved

1 tsp coconut oil

1 tbsp Midlife Curry Paste, see page 34

1 tsp runny honey

1 tbsp water

4 shallots, finely sliced

a squeeze of lemon juice

100g fresh coconut, grated

50g roasted, unsalted peanuts, crushed

a pinch of sea salt flakes

Cook the green beans in a saucepan of boiling water for a few minutes until just cooked but still *al dente*. Drain, then plunge them into a bowl of cold water (this will help retain their colour and crunch). Drain well and pat dry with kitchen paper.

Heat the coconut oil in a frying pan, add the curry paste and honey and fry gently for 2–3 minutes. Add the water and cook for a further few minutes. Transfer the paste mixture to a bowl and leave to cool slightly.

Combine the just-cooked beans, the shallots, lemon juice and grated coconut in a serving bowl, add the paste mixture and toss well. Season and sprinkle with the crushed peanuts, then serve.

Health Tip
Green beans contain a good amount of folate, a B vitamin that is important for the production of the feel-good hormones serotonin, dopamine and norepinephrine, regulators of mood, sleep and even appetite.

WHY WE LOVE IT

If you lined up all the world's veggies in order of their nutritional clout, broccoli would take the top spot. Beyond its impeccable health profile, broccoli is easy to prep, inexpensive and versatile – and it responds well to a bit of primping. Here, you get added nutritional value from lemon zest, chilli, mustard seeds and our fabulous Midlife Dukkah, which really is a mega-food in its own right. We also like the fact that you can make this in advance and set it aside. That's the Midlife Kitchen message in a single mouthful.

MIND, MEMORY & MOOD

DIGESTIVE HEALTH

HEART HEALTH

BLOOD-SUGAR BALANCE

BONE & JOINT HEALTH

HORMONE HARMONY

SKIN, SENSES & IMMUNITY

ENERGY BOOSTING

Zesty Tenderstem

WITH MIDLIFE DUKKAH & CHILLI

SERVES 4

200–250g Tenderstem broccoli, trimmed

a drizzle of extra virgin olive oil

2 tbsp Midlife Dukkah, see page 30

1 tsp mustard seeds

1 small red chilli, deseeded and finely sliced, or to taste

zest of 1 lemon

sea salt flakes and freshly ground black pepper

Cook the broccoli in a saucepan of boiling water for 2 minutes. It should be *al dente*, so take care not to overcook it. Drain, then plunge it into a bowl of very cold water (this will help retain its colour and crunch). Drain well and pat dry with kitchen paper.

Transfer the broccoli to a serving bowl, drizzle with a little olive oil and sprinkle over the dukkah, mustard seeds, chilli and lemon zest. Season and serve at room temperature.

Health Tip
A diet rich in cruciferous vegetables such as broccoli has been shown to help guard against many chronic diseases associated with ageing. Broccoli is also a good source of fibre and flavonols, which can reduce the risk of breast cancer.

WHY WE LOVE IT

A proper Makhani dhal is a rich, unctuous bowl of lentil-y bliss and we genuinely feel that there are times when the full butter and cream version is exactly what you are after. For day-to-day eating, though, a lighter option is welcome – so here we provide a luxe and a lean version. There's enough depth and layering of flavour in either if you want to make this a meal in itself, with a wholemeal pitta or one of our Easy Chapatis on the side.

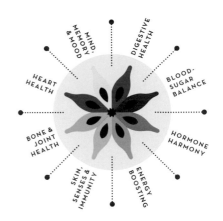

MIND, MEMORY & MOOD · DIGESTIVE HEALTH · BLOOD-SUGAR BALANCE · HORMONE HARMONY · ENERGY BOOSTING · SKIN, SENSES & IMMUNITY · BONE & JOINT HEALTH · HEART HEALTH

Luxe or Lean Makhani Dhal

SERVES 4

400g can kidney beans, drained and rinsed

40g butter (luxe) or 1 tbsp coconut oil (lean)

2 small red onions, diced

1 large green chilli, deseeded and sliced

2cm piece of fresh root ginger, peeled and finely grated

3 garlic cloves, thinly sliced

1/2–1 tsp hot chilli powder, to taste

2 tsp ground turmeric

1 tbsp ground cumin

1 tbsp ground coriander

1 tsp garam masala

4 cardamom pods, crushed

400ml vegetable or chicken stock

2 bay leaves

250g pouch ready-cooked Beluga lentils

1 ripe tomato, finely diced

sea salt flakes and freshly ground black pepper

3 tbsp double cream (luxe) or 3 tbsp natural yogurt (lean)

a handful of coriander leaves

Easy Chapatis, see page 206, or wholemeal pitta breads, to serve

Tip the kidney beans into a bowl and mash lightly with a fork. Set aside.

Heat the butter or coconut oil in a saucepan, add the onions and chilli and fry gently for 5 minutes until softened. Add the ginger, garlic, chilli powder and spices and cook for a further minute or two.

Add the water, the bay leaves, mashed beans, lentils and tomato. Bring to a simmer and cook for about 20 minutes, or until thickened.

Season with salt and pepper, then add the cream or yogurt and stir well. Scatter with the coriander, then serve with chapatis or pittas.

Midlife Hack: It's worth making a double batch of this as it freezes brilliantly – or add vegetable stock to turn it into a hearty soup, then just heat and eat.

Health Tip
Kidney beans are mighty big on fibre, which is key for keeping your digestive system in tip-top condition, and with their dark red skins, they're rich in cell-protecting antioxidants too.

WHY WE LOVE IT

Roasting whole garlic sweetens and mellows its flavour and produces an unctuous stickiness that makes for a delicious spread or topping. New-season garlic will give you the finest result.

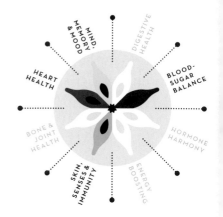

Roasted Garlic...

AND PLENTY OF WAYS TO USE IT

MAKES 6

6 good, fat garlic bulbs, outer leaves removed

1 tbsp extra virgin olive oil

sea salt flakes and freshly ground black pepper

Preheat the oven to 180°C/Gas Mark 4.

Slice off the tops of the garlic and place in a small roasting tin. Drizzle with the olive oil, season and cover with foil. Roast for 30–40 minutes until the garlic is butter-soft and golden.

Serve whole as a side dish, or squeeze the cloves to release the glory within.

Try This...
* Mashed into a salad dressing for a smooth, sweet flavour
* Squeezed into soups, sauces and stews for added savoury depth
* Swirled through mashed potato, sweet potato or White Bean Mash, see page 205
* Spread as a first layer on any Midlife Avo Toast, see pages 60–65
* Stirred through steamed asparagus or fine green beans
* Squeezed over roasted veg
* Mashed into softened butter with some chopped parsley, for a great garlic butter to add to steaks or bread
* Added to natural yogurt for a delicious dip
* Rubbed on to corn on the cob with a smear of butter

Midlife Hack: It's worth throwing a couple of garlic bulbs into the tin whenever you roast meat, ready to flavour the gravy for Sunday lunch.

Health Tip
Garlic is full of Midlife beauty, including vitamin B6, which enables the energy in food to be utilized by the body, making it great for keeping energy levels up. It also boosts the immune system and helps reduce blood pressure.

WHY WE LOVE IT

'Mata sapi' means bull's eye, which is how Indonesians describe a fried egg, but this is no ordinary egg. Cumin is in the spotlight here, the fragrant seeds decorating our bull's eye and the ground version flavouring the dressing, which, all in all, transforms a pouch of mixed grains into a mouth-watering mini-meal.

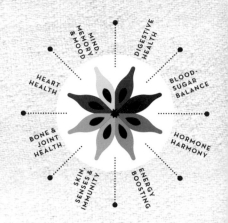

Mixed Grain Mata Sapi

SERVES 2

250g pouch ready-cooked mixed grains

a handful of coriander leaves, chopped

a handful of mint leaves, chopped

2 spring onions, finely sliced

50g feta cheese, crumbled

freshly ground black pepper

light olive oil spray

2 tsp cumin seeds

2 eggs

3 tbsp natural yogurt

1 tsp ground cumin

4 tbsp Wholly Guacamole, see page 220, or 1 ripe avocado, peeled, stoned and diced

Place the mixed grains in a large bowl and fluff up with a fork. Add the herbs, spring onions and feta and season well with pepper (using feta means that you shouldn't need to add salt).

Heat a large nonstick frying pan and spray with a little olive oil. Add the cumin seeds and cook for a couple of minutes until they start to colour and pop, taking care not to burn them, then remove from the pan. Fry the eggs, sunny side up, sprinkling with the toasted cumin seeds as they cook.

Meanwhile, combine the yogurt and ground cumin in a small bowl, then add to the grain mixture, mixing well.

Divide the grains between 2 shallow bowls, add 2 spoonfuls of Wholly Guacamole or half the avocado to each bowl and top with the cumin-fried eggs.

Health Tip

Whole grains are an essential part of a healthy diet in midlife. A large study, looking at data from 786,000 individuals, found that people who ate 70g of whole grains a day had a 22 per cent lower risk of mortality compared with those who ate few or no whole grains.

WHY WE LOVE IT

This is proper Midlife comfort food – satisfying, tasty and off-the-charts good for you. With your quinoa pouch to hand you can have this on the table in about 10 minutes, and it works well hot or cold, so any leftovers happily serve as tomorrow's lunch.

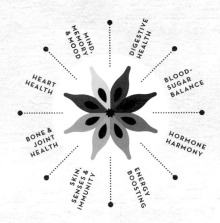

Red & White Quinoa
WITH MUSHROOMS, RED CHARD & PARMESAN

SERVES 4

1 tsp butter

1 tsp olive oil

200g chestnut or button mushrooms, sliced

250g pouch ready-cooked red and white quinoa

100g red chard, tough stems removed

a handful of mint leaves, chopped

a handful of flat leaf parsley, chopped

juice of ½ a lemon

1 tbsp natural yogurt

1 tsp grainy mustard

50g Parmesan cheese, grated, plus shavings to serve

sea salt flakes and freshly ground black pepper

Heat the butter and olive oil in a large frying pan, add the mushrooms and fry gently for a few minutes until softened and starting to brown. Add the quinoa, chard and herbs and cook for 3–4 minutes until the leaves have wilted.

Combine the lemon juice, yogurt and mustard in a bowl, then stir into the quinoa. Remove the pan from the heat, mix in the Parmesan, season well and serve with extra Parmesan shavings on top.

Health Tip
Unsurprisingly, red and white quinoa have very similar nutritional profiles, but red quinoa has extra riboflavin (vitamin B2), which works as an antioxidant to help prevent cell damage.

WHY WE LOVE IT

As you might expect, Beluga lentils are named after the caviar they resemble – we adore them because they're such a beautiful jet black, and they have a rich flavour and velvety texture that works perfectly in this good-carb bowl. Like all lentils, they're high in protein and fibre, so they make for a filling meal, particularly when paired with roasted sweet potato, toasted pine nuts and this sweet, dark dressing.

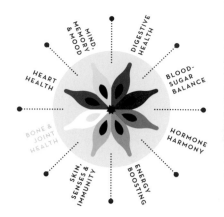

Black Beluga Lentils
WITH SWEET POTATO, BALSAMIC & POMEGRANATE

SERVES 4

1 sweet potato, about 250g, peeled and sliced

1 tsp olive oil

sea salt flakes and freshly ground black pepper

250g pouch ready-cooked Beluga or Puy lentils

1 small red onion, very finely diced

1 tbsp toasted pine nuts

a handful of pomegranate seeds

FOR THE DRESSING

1 tbsp balsamic vinegar

1 tbsp pomegranate molasses

1 tbsp extra virgin olive oil

1 tsp date syrup

Preheat the oven to 200°C/Gas Mark 6. Place the sweet potato slices in a small roasting tin, drizzle with the olive oil and season with salt and pepper. Bake for 10 minutes until just softened and starting to brown. Leave to cool, then cut or tear into 1cm pieces.

Tip the lentils into a serving bowl, add the cooled sweet potato and the onion.

Combine all the dressing ingredients in a bowl and stir well, then season. Pour half of the dressing over the lentils and toss together.

Top the lentils with the toasted pine nuts and pomegranate seeds and serve with the remaining dressing on the side.

Midlife Hack: Use the lentil and sweet potato mix (undressed) as the base for a stunning soup – just add veg stock, heat through and blend.

Health Tip
Unlike green lentils, black lentils possess anthocyanins, the same potent antioxidants found in dark berries such as blueberries and blackberries, offering added protection against age-related disease.

WHY WE LOVE IT

Almost too pretty to eat, this super side takes rice to another level with the addition of the bright greens and pinks of sweet broad beans, peas, crisp radish and spring onion. We quite like the name too....Try it with a combination of rices – the ready-cooked wild and wholegrain rice pouches come in handy here, although they generally already contain some oil, so taste first to get the balance right. Top with shredded cooked chicken if you're after a more substantial meal.

Midlife Rices

SERVES 4

100g fresh or frozen broad beans

100g frozen petits pois

250g pouch ready-cooked wholegrain, wild or black and red rice, or 150g wholegrain or wild rice, cooked and cooled

1 ripe avocado, peeled, stoned and sliced

10 long radishes, thinly sliced

3 spring onions, thinly sliced on the diagonal

a small handful of flat leaf parsley, chopped

sea salt flakes and freshly ground black pepper

FOR THE DRESSING

1 tbsp extra virgin olive oil

finely grated zest and juice of 1 lime

1 tsp chilli flakes

1 garlic clove, crushed

sea salt flakes and freshly ground black pepper

Cook the broad beans and peas in a saucepan of boiling water for 3 minutes until tender. Drain and refresh in cold water. Pop the beans from their outer skins and transfer to a serving bowl with the peas.

Combine all the dressing ingredients in a bowl and stir well.

Add all the remaining ingredients to the peas and beans, add the dressing and stir gently to combine. Season and serve.

Health Tip
Wholegrain rice is not milled, which means it retains much of its constituent B vits and essential minerals, together with lots of lovely fibre and fatty acids. Replacing white rice in your diet with an unrefined variety is good for the heart and may reduce the risk of developing type 2 diabetes.

WHY WE LOVE IT

It's so vividly, vibrantly green that you can just tell that this sublime mash-up of peas and beans is packed with goodies. What you get for a bit of effort shelling the broad beans is a supremely versatile crush: brilliant served warm beside grilled lamb chops or cold as a salad at a barbecue, it works equally well as a great dip or as a spread for bruschetta and crostini – although there's a real risk you'll polish this off before it even hits the table.

Broad Bean, Pea & Mint Smash

SERVES 4

150g fresh or frozen broad beans

150g frozen peas

sea salt flakes

1 small garlic clove, peeled and halved

a handful of mint leaves

2 tsp extra virgin olive oil

a squeeze of lemon juice

freshly ground black pepper

Cook the broad beans and peas in a saucepan of salted boiling water for 3 minutes until tender. Drain and refresh in cold water. Spend a mellow moment removing the white outer shells of the broad beans to get at the vivid green beans within.

Put three-quarters of the peas and beans into a food processor with the garlic, mint leaves, olive oil and lemon juice. Season well and blitz to a coarse pesto texture.

Transfer to a bowl and stir in the remaining whole peas and beans. Serve either warmed through or at room temperature.

Try This...
* Topped with a scatter of pine nuts or crumbled feta cheese
* Sprinkled with grated Parmesan and chilli flakes for a jumped-up version

Health Tip
Low-GI broad beans are a good source of protein, fibre and vitamins A and C; they also contain L-dopa, a chemical the body uses to produce dopamine. So they could make you feel good too!

WHY WE LOVE IT

This is truly a mash made in heaven. In fact, it's a mash made in the Midlife Kitchen, so you know it's going to be bursting with good things and utterly delicious to boot. It is fabulous served hot with fish (a piece of poached smoked haddock on top would be lovely) – or try it chilled as a dip, or as a protein-packed, slow-burn, tasty topping for Seedy Soda Bread, see page 209. The riffs on this theme are endless, so we've included some of our best variations below.

MIND MEMORY & MOOD · DIGESTIVE HEALTH · BLOOD-SUGAR BALANCE · HORMONE HARMONY · ENERGY BOOSTING · SKIN, SENSES & IMMUNITY · BONE & JOINT HEALTH · HEART HEALTH

White Bean Mash
WITH LEMON & SAGE

SERVES 2

2 tbsp extra virgin olive oil

3 garlic cloves, crushed

10 sage leaves, finely sliced

400g can white beans (try cannellini or butter beans), drained and rinsed

3 tbsp water

2 tbsp natural yogurt

a squeeze of lemon juice

zest of ½ a lemon

sea salt flakes and freshly ground black pepper

Health Tip
Early research suggests that fresh sage can be effective in treating symptoms of the menopause, especially hot flushes.

Heat the olive oil, garlic and sage in a medium saucepan over a low heat and cook for a minute or so until the garlic has softened. Add the beans and mash lightly with a fork.

Add the water, bring to a simmer, then cook for 3–4 minutes until the liquid has reduced almost completely. Remove the pan from the heat and set aside.

Mix the yogurt, lemon juice and zest in a bowl and season well (this benefits from plenty of black pepper).

Stir the yogurt mixture through the beans and serve. The mash will keep in the fridge for several days.

Try This...
Replace the garlic, sage and lemon juice and zest with:

* 1 teaspoon of ground cumin, a handful of chopped coriander and the juice of 1 lime
* A handful of chopped tarragon and thyme and 1 teaspoon of grainy Dijon mustard
* 1 tablespoon of Midlife Dukkah, see page 30, and the juice of 1 lime
* A handful of chopped flat leaf parsley and a few soft Roasted Garlic cloves, see page 196

WHY WE LOVE IT

Our favourite flatbread is that basic of Indian cuisine: the humble chapati. Happily, they are also extremely easy to make, as neither of us are natural-born kneaders. This recipe is so ridiculously simple – a little flour, a splash of water, a mere 5 minutes' work – that you will feel a disproportionate amount of satisfaction as you tuck in to your own healthy homemade wraps.

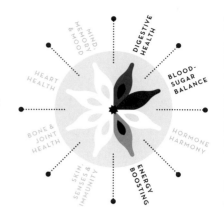

MIND, MEMORY & MOOD
DIGESTIVE HEALTH
HEART HEALTH
BLOOD-SUGAR BALANCE
BONE & JOINT HEALTH
HORMONE HARMONY
SKIN, SENSES & IMMUNITY
ENERGY BOOSTING

Easy Chapatis

MAKES 4

120g wholemeal flour
or half rye, half white flour,
plus extra for dusting

a pinch of sea salt flakes

100ml lukewarm water

light olive oil spray

Health Tip
We generally use wholemeal flour in the Midlife Kitchen because it includes the highly nutritious bran and germ of the wheat grain, source of most of the vitamins, minerals and fibre found in flour.

Sift the flour into a bowl, adding any fibre that remains in the sieve. Add the salt, then slowly incorporate the water with your hands to make a soft dough. Knead for a minute or two on a lightly oiled surface to make a smooth and pliable ball. The longer you knead, the softer the chapatis will be, but there is no need to knead for more than a couple of minutes. Cover the dough with a damp cloth or clingfilm and leave to rest for at least 10 minutes.

Divide the dough into 4 equal pieces, then roll into smooth balls and press flat. Press both sides of the flattened balls on to a floured surface (this makes them easier to roll), then roll out each ball to form a 25cm-diameter circle (they should be quite thin – just a millimetre or two).

Heat a large nonstick frying pan over a high heat and spray with olive oil. Place a chapati in the pan and spray the top of the chapati with a little more oil.

When it starts to puff up, flip it (there will be some golden brown spots on the cooked side).

Using a spatula, press lightly on the puffed parts, cooking for a further minute until it has light golden brown spots on both sides. Remove from the pan and repeat with the remaining chapatis.

Serve immediately. Alternatively, if you make a big batch, they will keep for a couple of days in an airtight container in the fridge. Simply reheat in a frying pan to serve.

WHY WE LOVE IT

We'd love to be bread makers, really we would – the smell of freshly baked dough, flour up to our elbows, shafts of light through the farmhouse windows... the reality is, however, that very few of us (and absolutely neither of us) have the time or the inclination to embark on proper yeast–knead–prove bread making, especially when the end product lasts for half a day before turning into a doorstop. So this is the bread we swear by – a simple soda bread with a Midlife seedy twist. This excellent healthy loaf can be on the table within half an hour; better yet, it's impossible to muck up.

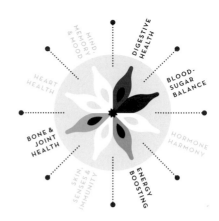

Seedy Soda Bread

MAKES 1 LOAF

225g wholemeal flour, plus extra for dusting

225g plain flour

1 tsp caster sugar

1 tsp bicarbonate of soda

½ tsp sea salt flakes

3 tbsp Midlife Raw Seed Mix, see page 25, or 2 tbsp sunflower seeds and 1 tbsp pumpkin seeds

200g natural yogurt

200ml milk

2 tsp rolled oats

Preheat the oven to 200°C/Gas Mark 6. Place a lidded casserole dish in the oven to warm.

Place all the dry ingredients in a large bowl and mix together. Add the yogurt and milk and combine to make a soft, pliable dough, gathering any escaping seeds back into the mix.

Working quickly, shape into a round loaf and carefully place in the hot casserole, topping with a little more flour. Using a sharp knife, score the top with a cross and scatter with the oats.

Replace the lid and bake for 20 minutes, then remove the lid and bake for a further 5 minutes until nutty brown. When the bread is cooked, it should sound hollow when tapped on the base.

Turn out and leave to cool slightly before tucking in.

Health Tip
This loaf contains plenty of insoluble fibre, traditionally known as roughage, which passes through the body almost undigested. Foods rich in insoluble fibre not only fill you up, but also keep things trucking through the digestive system.

WHY WE LOVE IT

'Sooooooo good!' That's what our families think of this yummy snack mix. We love a Snickers bar, but they have now been replaced in our hearts by this far healthier grown-up reinvention. The familiar peanuty, chocolatey flavours are there, and we've added Brazils and walnuts, which add up to a nutritious, energy-packed snack.

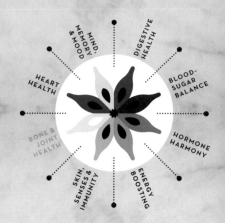

Midlife Mega Mix
WITH PEANUTS & DARK CHOCOLATE

MAKES 200G

75g roasted, salted peanuts

50g walnut pieces

25g Brazil nuts, each chopped into 3 pieces

50g organic dark chocolate chips

Combine all the ingredients, then store in an airtight container. The mix will keep for weeks, but honestly it won't hang around that long!

Midlife Hack: Look for a 'bitter-sweet' choc chip containing 70% cocoa solids. Some choc chips contain stabilizers to allow them to retain their shape in cooking, which can make them taste waxy, so choose your chips with care.

Health Tip
Nuts contain protein, fibre and healthy fats, but they're calorific, too (the NHS recommends half a handful a day as the optimum portion size). Brazils bring selenium to this mix – great for balancing mood, slowing the ageing of the skin and enhancing thyroid function.

WHY WE LOVE IT

As you might have noticed, we're nuts about nuts in the Midlife Kitchen. They're our go-to high-protein snack when we are having a busy day. A small handful will stave off hunger pangs and keep your energy and blood-sugar levels on an even keel. This mix is equally awesome for breakfast, scattered over Midlife Yogurt and chopped fruit.

MIND, MEMORY & MOOD

DIGESTIVE HEALTH

HEART HEALTH

BLOOD-SUGAR BALANCE

BONE & JOINT HEALTH

HORMONE HARMONY

SKIN, SENSES & IMMUNITY

ENERGY BOOSTING

Midlife Toasted Trail Mix

MAKES 500G

300g shelled nuts, choose from: walnuts, Brazils, peanuts, cashews, almonds, hazelnuts, pistachios, coconut chips

100g dried fruit, choose from: apricots, figs, raisins, dates, pineapple, mango, pear, apple, cranberries, goji berries, blueberries, cherries

100g seeds, choose from: pumpkin seeds, sunflower seeds, sesame seeds, flaxseed

2 tbsp coconut oil, melted if solid

2 tsp ground cinnamon

a grind of vanilla bean, see Midlife Hack, or ½ tsp vanilla extract

Health Tip
There is overwhelming evidence that people who regularly eat nuts and seeds have a lower risk of developing heart disease, type 2 diabetes and obesity.

Preheat the oven to 160°C/Gas Mark 3. Line a large baking tray with nonstick baking paper.

Chop the larger ingredients (Brazil nuts, walnuts, apricots and figs) into smaller pieces, aiming for 1cm pieces.

Put the nuts, seeds and dried fruit into a bowl. Add the coconut oil, cinnamon and vanilla and mix well. Spread the mixture out on the prepared baking tray and bake for 20 minutes until crisp and golden, turning the mixture after 10 minutes.

Leave the mix to cool, then store in an airtight container for up to 1 week.

Midlife Hack: We often use a vanilla bean grinder rather than a whole pod, essence or extract – it's the quickest way to add pretty flecks of vanilla to porridge, yogurt or bakes.

WHY WE LOVE IT

Our perennial dilemma is what to eat when the Midlife munchies call; we're looking for sweet, salty, crunchy and spicy... but ultimately healthy. Here, we square the circle by coating almonds – full of protein, fibre, vitamin E, essential minerals and antioxidants – with an irresistible combination of super spices and a touch of honey, crisped to perfection in the oven.

Hot Tapas Almonds

WITH HONEY & CINNAMON

MAKES 200G

light olive oil spray

2 tsp ground cumin

1 tsp ground cinnamon

¼ tsp cayenne pepper, or more to taste

½ tsp sea salt flakes

200g whole almonds, with skins on

1 tbsp runny honey

Preheat the oven to 180°C/Gas Mark 4. Line a baking tray with nonstick baking paper and spray with a little olive oil.

Combine the spices and salt in a bowl. Put the almonds into another bowl, drizzle with the honey and mix well to ensure they are all coated. Add the spice mixture and stir until the almonds are evenly coated.

Spread out the almonds on the prepared baking tray and bake for 25 minutes until crisp and golden, turning the nuts after about 15 minutes to prevent them sticking.

Leave to cool for 20 minutes before serving, or cool completely and store in an airtight container for up to 1 week.

Health Tip
Whole almonds, including the skins, are loaded with flavonoids – plant nutrients that are key to maintaining a healthy heart and protecting the body from the effects of ageing.

WHY WE LOVE IT

If you fancy a healthy little savoury something to accompany a good glass of wine, these excellent cheesy biscuits do the business. They're buttery and crunchy, as is only fitting for a shortbread, but they also contain a decent haul of Midlife goodness – from the olive oil, pistachios, almonds and mustard to the sesame seeds, cumin seeds, dried oregano or chilli flakes used as a topping.

Parmesan, Almond & Pistachio Sables

MAKES 30

100g Parmesan cheese, grated

50g blanched almonds

50g pistachio nuts

100g butter, softened

50ml extra virgin olive oil

50g semolina

100g self-raising flour

1 heaped tsp English mustard powder

sea salt flakes and freshly ground black pepper

FOR THE TOPPINGS

crushed pistachio nuts

sesame seeds, poppy seeds and/or cumin seeds

dried oregano and/or chilli flakes

Health Tip
The unique green and purple colour of the pistachio kernel is a result of its lutein and anthocyanin content. Lutein is often referred to as the 'eye vitamin' as it can help prevent eye problems including age-related macular degeneration.

Preheat the oven to 180°C/Gas Mark 4. Line a large baking sheet with nonstick baking paper.

Place all the ingredients, except for the toppings, in a food processor and whizz to form a coarse dough. Tip the dough on to a piece of clingfilm and shape into a long sausage, using the film to help with the rolling. Secure the ends of the roll and place in the freezer for at least 30 minutes.

When chilled, use a sharp knife and slice the dough into slim discs about 3mm thick.

Place the discs on the prepared baking sheet and sprinkle over the toppings of your choice (some of each looks pretty). Bake for 15 minutes until golden brown and crisp. Transfer to a wire rack and leave to cool.

The sables will keep for up to 2 days in an airtight container.

Midlife Hack: Keep the dough 'sausage' in the freezer and it will be ready to bake at a moment's notice if you need a quick savoury snack for parties.

WHY WE LOVE IT

Not really a recipe, just a really good idea. Chop some of your favourite fruit, add a few berries and a handful of dates and pop the lot in the freezer. Then later, when you need a sweet fix, you have lovely chewy chunks of fruity goodness. Needless to say, this is universally adored by kids too.

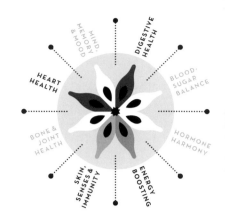

Freezer Fruit

**MAKES AS MUCH
AS YOU LIKE!**

mixed fruit, such as banana, mango, papaya, pineapple and kiwifruit, cut into bite-sized chunks

mixed whole fruit, such as blueberries, raspberries and grapes

pitted Medjool dates

Put your selection of fruit in a plastic container and freeze for a few hours or overnight.

Eat straight from the freezer.

Try This...
* As a fruit smoothie, combined with natural yogurt or a splash of coconut water

Health Tip
Some people think that because added sugars are bad for you, the same must apply to fruit. While fruit *does* contain fructose, it is also packaged with fibre and a host of vital nutrients, making it a natural, healthy snack.

MIDLIFE
EXTRAS

WHY WE LOVE IT

This super spread does the job of hummus but with a Midlife twist – replacing the more usual chickpeas with butter beans and spinach to give a lighter texture. We've kept it simple, so you can whizz it up at a moment's notice to have on stand-by in the fridge. It's perfect as a dip for raw veggies, or spread thickly on toast topped with a handful of Midlife Spiced Seed Mix, see page 26.

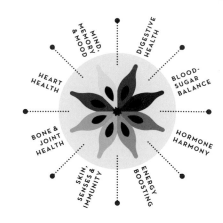

Middle-aged Spread

MAKES 500G

250g spinach leaves

400g can butter beans, drained and rinsed

2 tbsp extra virgin olive oil

juice of 1/2 a lemon

a small handful of flat leaf parsley, roughly chopped

1 tbsp Midlife Spice Mix, see page 24, or 1 tsp ground coriander and 1 tsp ground cumin

2 tbsp natural yogurt

1 garlic clove, crushed

sea salt flakes and freshly ground black pepper

Rinse the spinach, then cook in a large frying pan with the residual water over a low heat for 2 minutes until wilted. Drain well and pat dry with kitchen paper to remove any moisture.

Put the spinach into a food processor, add the remaining ingredients and pulse to a semi-smooth texture.

This can be served warm, or cold from the fridge, where it will keep in an airtight container for up to a week.

Health Tip
Butter beans are the star here, providing protein, healthy carbs and a brilliant fibre fix. This benefits the cardiovascular and digestive systems, as well as priming energy levels.

WHY WE LOVE IT

We might just have created the ultimate dip. But it's not just a dip, it's a spread, it's a sauce, it's breakfast, lunch and dinner. As we know, avocados are positively full of the good stuff – but we've added so much more to this that you *need* to have it in your fridge: seeds, peas, edamame, mint, lime juice, garlic... it's a roll call of Midlife excellence.

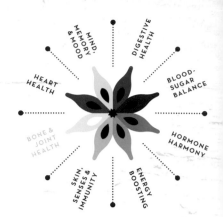

Wholly Guacamole

MAKES 500G

100g frozen edamame beans

100g frozen peas

3 tbsp Midlife Raw Seed Mix, see page 25, or pumpkin seeds

2 perfectly ripe avocados

2 garlic cloves, crushed

2 spring onions, sliced

a handful of mint leaves, chopped

a handful of flat leaf parsley, chopped

juice of 2 limes

finely grated zest of 1 lime

2 tbsp extra virgin olive oil

1/2 tsp sea salt flakes

freshly ground black pepper

1 ripe tomato, finely diced

Cook the edamame beans and peas in a saucepan of boiling water for 3 minutes until tender. Drain and refresh in cold water. Pop the beans from their outer skins and set aside with the peas.

Place the seed mix in a small, shallow frying pan and dry-fry over a medium heat for a few minutes until just starting to colour and pop, taking care not to burn them. Leave to cool for a few minutes, then tip into a coffee grinder or spice mill and pulse until coarsely ground. Alternatively, pound the seeds using a pestle and mortar.

Peel and stone the avocados, then put into a food processor with the ground seeds. Add all the remaining ingredients, except the tomato, and pulse to a semi-chunky texture. Add the diced tomato and stir well. Transfer the guacamole to a bowl and chill for 30 minutes before serving.

Try This...
* As a sauce for pan-fried fish or fishcakes
* As a dip for toasted pitta bread with crumbled feta cheese
* As a base for Avo Toast, see pages 60–65
* Spooned on to an omelette

Midlife Hack: Fresh shelled edamame beans are available at most supermarkets; just boil for a few minutes and they are ready to go.

Health Tip
Studies show that eating avocados can help lower heart- disease risk factors, improving your cholesterol profile as well as lowering blood triglycerides.

WHY WE LOVE IT

Hummus is a reliable staple in the fridges of the nation; we know it's a fine thing because it's full of plant protein, fibre and lip-smacking flavour. But the commercial versions are often dosed with high levels of salt (research recently found that some pots contain as much salt as four bags of crisps), while you can't always be sure of the quality of oil that goes in. Making your own is the answer. In this case, there's added buzz from roasted red peppers, almonds and paprika, and only as much salt as you choose to add.

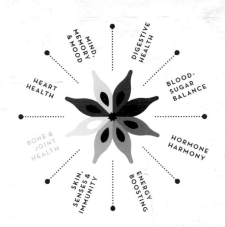

MIND, MEMORY & MOOD

DIGESTIVE HEALTH

HEART HEALTH

BLOOD-SUGAR BALANCE

BONE & JOINT HEALTH

HORMONE HARMONY

SKIN, SENSES & IMMUNITY

ENERGY BOOSTING

Roasted Red Pepper Hummus

WITH ALMONDS & SMOKED PAPRIKA

MAKES 500G

1 large red pepper

400g can chickpeas, drained and rinsed

2 tbsp Midlife LSA, see page 27, or ground almonds

2 tbsp tahini

2 tbsp extra virgin olive oil

2 tbsp lemon juice

3 tbsp warm water

1 garlic clove, crushed

1 tsp smoked paprika

sea salt flakes and freshly ground black pepper

Cook the red pepper under a preheated hot grill for 5 minutes, turning occasionally, until softened and slightly charred. Leave to cool a little, then remove the stalk, deseed and roughly chop.

Place the red pepper in a food processor, add the remaining ingredients and pulse to a coarse paste (or make it smoother if you prefer).

The hummus will keep in an airtight container in the fridge for up to 3 days.

Health Tip
100g of red pepper contains more than three times the recommended dietary allowance (RDA) for vitamin C, making it one of the richest sources of this essential nutrient, vital for cell protection and immunity.

WHY WE LOVE IT

If you're looking for a quick lunch, this healthy fallback recipe is simply delicious. The oily fish provides omega-3s, there's vitamin C from the dill, lemon juice and zest, and excellent digestive benefits from the yogurt. Add chilli flakes if you like a kick. Be warned though, it's addictive!

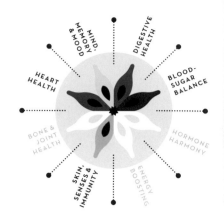

Smoked Mackerel & Dill Pâté

SERVES 2

300g smoked mackerel fillets, skin removed

2 tbsp thick Greek yogurt

finely grated zest and juice of ½ a lemon

1 spring onion, finely sliced

a handful of dill, chopped

sea salt flakes and freshly ground black pepper

½ tsp chilli flakes (optional)

Place the mackerel fillets in a bowl and mash gently with a fork. Add the remaining ingredients and mix well. Alternatively, if you prefer a smoother pâté, whizz the ingredients together in a food processor.

Chill for at least 30 minutes before serving. This works wonderfully as a dip for veggies, on toasted Seedy Soda Bread, see page 209, or with oatcakes.

The pâté will keep in the fridge for several days.

Health Tip
We ❤ oily fish and, happily, oily fish loves your ❤. Studies have found that eating oily fish can lower blood pressure and reduce fat build-up in the arteries.

WHY WE LOVE IT

This five-minute wonder, stacked with must-have omega-3s, makes a lovely light starter served on warm crisp wholemeal toast, grainy bagels or rye bread, or a healthy canapé spread on to pumpernickel rye toasts. You want a pungent punch of fresh horseradish here, while plenty of black pepper, snipped chives and antioxidant lemon zest make it a truly magic mouthful.

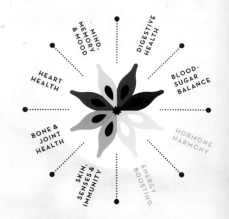

Smoked Trout Pâté

WITH LEMON & HORSERADISH

SERVES 4

300g hot-smoked trout fillets, skin removed

2 tbsp natural yogurt

2 tsp fresh horseradish root, peeled and grated, or ready-grated horseradish in a jar (not horseradish sauce)

grated zest and juice of ½ a lemon

a pinch of sea salt flakes

freshly ground black pepper

1 tbsp snipped chives

Place 150g of the smoked trout in a food processor, add the yogurt, horseradish, lemon juice and zest. Season, then pulse until smooth.

Transfer to a bowl and break in the remaining fish. Add the chives and check the seasoning, then stir and serve.

Midlife Hack: Fresh horseradish root, like ginger or turmeric, freezes well. If you are having trouble finding fresh or grated horseradish, use English mustard instead.

Health Tip
Horseradish has long been used as a traditional remedy for sinusitis and colds, and recent research has indeed found that it has antibacterial properties to help fight infections naturally. One study from the University of Illinois indicated that the glucosinolates in horseradish could increase human resistance to cancer.

WHY WE LOVE IT

If there's one food that can really contribute to health in midlife, it has to be oily fish. Sardines may have fallen out of fashion, but they are a nutritional knockout, almost a 'perfect food', with benefits for the entire body. So we've given these overlooked little fish an update in this rich, savoury pâté – just the thing for high tea, spread generously on warm toasted pitta bread triangles. They'd make an excellent canapé too.

MIND, MEMORY & MOOD

DIGESTIVE HEALTH

HEART HEALTH

BLOOD-SUGAR BALANCE

BONE & JOINT HEALTH

HORMONE HARMONY

SKIN, SENSES & IMMUNITY

ENERGY BOOSTING

Sardinade

SERVES 2

100g tin sardines in olive oil

½ a small red onion, very finely diced

a small handful of parsley, chopped

6 black Greek olives, pitted and finely chopped

juice of ½ a lemon

a few drops of Tabasco, or to taste

20g butter, melted

freshly ground black pepper

Drain the sardines, reserving 1 tablespoon of the oil. Place the fish in a bowl and mash well with a fork.

Add the onion, parsley, olives, lemon juice, Tabasco, reserved olive oil and half the melted butter. Season with black pepper and mix well.

Press the mixture into 2 ramekins and pour over the remaining butter. Chill for at least 30 minutes before serving. The sardinade will keep in the fridge for up to 3 days.

Midlife Hack: This dish works best with tinned sardines, which are a cheap store-cupboard staple in the Midlife Kitchen. Look for sardines in extra virgin olive oil – it will add to the omega-3 content of your pâté.

Health Tip
Small oily fish like sardines can be eaten whole, which provides maximum nutritional benefit, particularly good for the bones and joints. Sardines are very high in heart-healthy fatty acids, which have also been found to boost the brain and mood.

WHY WE LOVE IT

Uchucuta is the Peruvian equivalent of Argentinian chimichurri – a herby, garlicky sauce usually served with meat. This, however, includes cheese, which makes for a smoother and more complex sauce. In Peru, the cheese of choice is 'queso fresco' (fresh cheese); our nearest cousin is feta. Charring the chillies over a naked flame only takes a moment and introduces a warm, rounded note. The result is pretty fiery, so play around with the amount of chilli to suit your tolerance – we prefer to deseed the charred chillies to turn down the dial a bit.

Uchucuta

SERVES 5
MAKES APPROX. 250G

1 long green jalapeño chilli

1 Scotch bonnet chilli

150g feta cheese, crumbled

1 tbsp extra virgin olive oil

2 tbsp natural yogurt

a squeeze of lemon or lime juice

1 garlic clove, peeled and halved

a handful of flat leaf parsley, roughly chopped

a handful of coriander (leaves and stalks), roughly chopped

sea salt flakes and freshly ground black pepper

Cook the chillies under a preheated hot grill until slightly blackened and beginning to soften. Alternatively, using tongs, char over an open flame. Leave to cool, then remove the stalk and deseed, if you prefer a less intense heat.

Put the charred chillies and all the remaining ingredients into a food processor and blitz until smooth. Store in an airtight container in the fridge for up to 3 days.

Try This...

* As a marinade for a whole chicken
* As a fabulous dip for corn chips
* On a baked potato
* As a condiment to slop generously over barbecued meat
* For Uchucuta Pork, see page 178

See photograph on page 229.

Health Tip
The pungent heat of chillies comes from the plant alkaloid capsaicin, which has been shown to have cardio-protective and anti-inflammatory properties; it also has beneficial effects on the gastrointestinal system and can protect the fats in your blood from damage by free radicals.

WHY WE LOVE IT

We always love finding a new recipe that's healthy, easy and can be made in advance – and this one fits the bill perfectly. Matbucha is a versatile, lightly spiced Israeli tomato salad, usually eaten at room temperature as a side dish, spread or dip. The health heroes here are the tomatoes and red peppers, both of which are rich in lycopene, which protects the skin and supports healthy heart function.

Matbucha

ISRAELI SPICED TOMATO SALSA

SERVES 10
MAKES APPROX. 500G

1 tbsp extra virgin olive oil

3 garlic cloves, crushed

2 tsp Midlife Spice Mix, see page 24

a pinch of cayenne pepper

5 ripe tomatoes, roughly diced

1 large red chilli, deseeded and finely sliced (optional)

1 red pepper, cored, deseeded and roughly diced

sea salt flakes

Health Tip
Preliminary evidence from an extensive study in China found that those who regularly ate spicy foods, mainly coming from chilli, were found to have a 14 per cent lower mortality risk than those who rarely consumed such foods.

Heat the olive oil in a saucepan, add the garlic and fry gently for 1 minute, then stir in the spices and fry for a further 2 minutes.

Add the tomatoes, chilli (if using) and the red pepper, then pour in enough water to just cover the mix. Add a pinch of salt and bring to the boil. Reduce the heat to low and simmer gently for 1½ hours, stirring occasionally and adding more water if it becomes too thick. The final consistency should resemble a chunky salsa.

Matbucha is best served at room temperature, but it can be stored in the fridge for up to 3 days.

See photograph on page 229.

Midlife Hack: Matbucha makes an excellent bruschetta topping; try it on some lightly toasted Seedy Soda Bread, see page 209.

WHY WE LOVE IT

When we discovered 'mole verde', it quickly became a firm favourite at Midlife Central. For a start, it's based on three A* ingredients – broccoli, asparagus and pumpkin seeds – whizzed up with even more top-grade goodness from cumin, olive oil, chilli and a hint of garlic. But it's the flavour that makes this Mexican staple so addictive. It's rich, complex, sweet/savoury and almost nutty, bringing something seriously good to a meal.

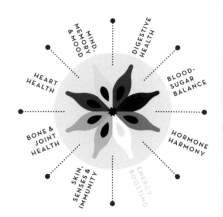

Mole Verde

SERVES 6
MAKES APPROX. 500G

6 fat asparagus spears, trimmed and roughly chopped

sea salt flakes

50g pumpkin seeds, plus extra to serve (optional)

1 tsp ground cumin

a pinch of ground cinnamon

2 tbsp olive oil

150g broccoli (including stalks), roughly chopped

1 banana shallot or ½ an onion, diced

225ml boiling water

a handful of coriander (leaves and stalks), roughly chopped

1 small green chilli, deseeded and roughly chopped

1 garlic clove, peeled and halved

freshly ground black pepper

cumin seeds, to serve (optional)

Health Tip
Pumpkin seeds, or *pepitas* in Spanish, contain a whole realm of nutrients, including protein, iron, vitamin K, magnesium and zinc – plus fibre and essential fatty acids, which support heart health. They contain phytoestrogens too, which have been found to help reduce menopause symptoms.

Cook the asparagus spears in a saucepan of salted boiling water for 1 minute until *al dente*. Drain, then plunge them into a bowl of cold water (this will help retain their colour). Drain well and pat dry with kitchen paper.

Place the pumpkin seeds, ground cumin and cinnamon in a large, shallow frying pan and dry-fry over a medium heat for 2–3 minutes until the seeds start to colour and pop, taking care not to burn them. Tip into a bowl and set aside.

Heat the olive oil in the pan, add the broccoli, shallot or onion and blanched asparagus and cook for 1 minute, stirring. Add the boiling water and simmer, uncovered, for 5 minutes, then stir in the coriander, chilli, garlic and spiced pumpkin seeds and cook for a further 5 minutes. Season to taste and leave to cool slightly.

Blend the vegetable mixture in a food processor or blender, then pour into a bowl and chill before serving. If you really can't wait, eat it warm from the bowl topped with extra pumpkin seeds and cumin seeds.

Try This...
* As a marinade for chicken
* With grilled meat or prawns
* As a dip with toasted pitta breads

Midlife Hack: With the addition of a little stock this makes a hearty, heart-loving and extremely tasty soup.

MATBUCHA

UCHUCUTA

MOLE VERDE

WHY WE LOVE IT

The astonishing pink of this raita will bring Midlife brilliance to the side of any plate, thanks to the abundant betacyanin, an antioxidant found in beetroot. The addition of aromatic garam masala, apple and fresh mint add extraordinary depth of flavour and even more nutritional rewards.

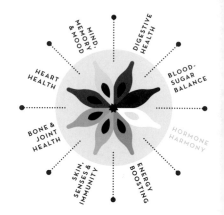

Beetroot Raita

WITH APPLE & GARAM MASALA

SERVES 5
MAKES APPROX. 250G

60g cooked beetroot, finely diced

150g thick Greek yogurt

1 heaped tsp garam masala

a small handful of mint leaves, finely sliced, plus extra to serve

1 tsp lemon juice

½ an apple, cored and grated

sea salt flakes and freshly ground black pepper

Combine all the ingredients in a bowl.

Chill for at least 30 minutes. Scatter with extra chopped mint and serve. The raita will keep in the fridge for up to 2 days.

Midlife Hack: A garam masala grinder, which contains the whole spices, will deliver a potent blast of fresh flavour every time.

Health Tip

Garam masala, a combination of cumin seeds, cinnamon, black pepper, nutmeg, cardamom and cloves, has traditionally been used in Ayurvedic medicine for its health-giving properties; indeed, there is some evidence to suggest it can aid digestion.

WHY WE LOVE IT

Taking a basic, like pesto, and reinventing it in the interests of better health is the name of the game in the Midlife Kitchen. To pimp our pesto we've used walnuts, which are excellent heart helpers, and watercress, a nutritional blockbuster that brings a peppery new bite to an old favourite.

Walnut, Watercress & Pecorino Pesto

SERVES 4 (WITH PASTA)

50g walnut pieces

1 small garlic clove, peeled and halved

2 tbsp extra virgin olive oil

zest and juice of ½ a lemon

150g watercress, rinsed

30g Pecorino cheese, grated

a small pinch of sea salt flakes

freshly ground black pepper

Put all the ingredients into a food processor and blitz to a coarse consistency.

Best served stirred through pasta the same day it's made, while the pesto is at its freshest.

Health Tip
A study in the American Journal of Clinical Nutrition found that consumption of watercress can be linked to a reduced risk of cancer via decreased damage to DNA.

WHY WE LOVE IT

This great pesto boasts gutsy powerhouse nutrients – from pumpkin, nuts, citrus and sage – which are all high in vitamins and antioxidants to help protect against colds and flu. Think of it as an immunity booster, to adorn an everyday pasta with good-for-you glory.

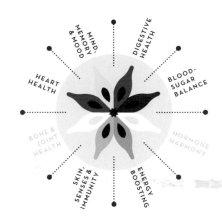

Pumpkin, Pecan & Sage Pesto

SERVES 6 (WITH PASTA)

50g pecan nuts

50g pumpkin seeds

200g canned pumpkin purée

30g Parmesan cheese, grated

juice of 1 lemon

1 tbsp extra virgin olive oil

sea salt flakes and freshly ground black pepper

10 sage leaves, finely sliced

Put the pecans and pumpkin seeds into a food processor and blitz to a coarse crumb. Add the pumpkin purée, Parmesan, lemon juice and olive oil and blitz again.

Transfer to a bowl, season and stir in the thin slivers of sage.

Serve stirred through your favourite pasta. The pesto can be stored in the fridge for up to 2 days.

Try This...
* On wholewheat linguine, topped with extra Parmesan and herbs
* As a filling for homemade ravioli, drizzled with warm sage butter

Health Tip
Pecans, along with walnuts, contain the highest antioxidant value of all edible nuts, and provide healthy fats to benefit the heart and brain. A recent study found that people who eat nuts daily are 20 per cent more likely to live longer (and are slimmer too).

WHY WE LOVE IT

If we had to shut our eyes and jot down the Midlife Kitchen's top-performing ingredients, the list would look a lot like...this recipe for Salsa Verde! Parsley is clearly the main event here, bolstered by a supporting cast of goodness from the apple cider vinegar, lemon juice, anchovies, mustard and garlic, resulting in a bold and brilliant spoonful. Purists argue that every ingredient in a salsa verde should be chopped by hand. Be our guest. If pushed for time, though, blitz away; you'll still get an authentic sauce – it will just be a little more uniform in texture.

MIND, MEMORY & MOOD

DIGESTIVE HEALTH

HEART HEALTH

BLOOD-SUGAR BALANCE

BONE & JOINT HEALTH

HORMONE HARMONY

SKIN, SENSES & IMMUNITY

ENERGY BOOSTING

Midlife Salsa Verde

SERVES 4
MAKES APPROX. 200G

a large handful of parsley

4 anchovy fillets, rinsed

1 tbsp capers, rinsed

1 garlic clove, peeled and quartered

4 tbsp extra virgin olive oil

1 tbsp lemon juice

grated zest of ½ a lemon

1 tsp apple cider vinegar

2 tsp Dijon mustard

freshly ground black pepper

Finely chop the parsley, anchovies, capers and garlic by hand, which gives a sauce with more texture, then transfer to a bowl. Add the olive oil, lemon juice and zest, vinegar and mustard and season with plenty of pepper.

Alternatively, blitz all the ingredients in a food processor. It's best served fresh, when the green colour is most vivid, but it will keep in the fridge for a couple of days.

Try This...
* As a dip for crusty bread
* Dolloped on to a baked sweet potato
* Drizzled over new potatoes
* Served with scrambled eggs
* The classic Italian way, served alongside grilled or poached fish

See photograph on page 237.

Midlife Hack: This also works well with other soft herbs, such as mint, tarragon or basil.

Health Tip
Parsley is a good source of vitamins A, C and K, plus folate and iron – delivering bags of goodies to support immunity, bones, joints and skin. But why stop there? It's also loaded with phytochemicals, flavonoids and antioxidants.

WHY WE LOVE IT

Of all the lovely foods we have discovered in Bali this is our absolute favourite. It's the ultimate pick-me-up for any simply grilled piece of meat or fish – a heady combination of lemon grass, chilli, lime and terasi shrimp paste, the Indonesian equivalent of Thai fish sauce (which you can use instead, if terasi eludes you).

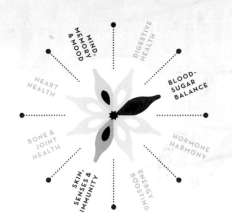

MIND, MEMORY & MOOD

DIGESTIVE HEALTH

HEART HEALTH

BLOOD-SUGAR BALANCE

BONE & JOINT HEALTH

HORMONE HARMONY

SKIN, SENSES & IMMUNITY

ENERGY BOOSTING

Sambal Matah

SERVES 3
MAKES APPROX. 150G

3-4 shallots, peeled and finely chopped

1 spring onion, finely chopped

2 small red chillies, deseeded and finely chopped

2 lemon grass stalks, tough outer layers removed, finely minced

½ tsp terasi shrimp paste or Thai fish sauce (nam pla)

2 tbsp olive oil

juice of 2 limes

a pinch of sea salt flakes

Combine all the ingredients in a bowl. Leave to stand for 10 minutes or so to allow the flavours to marry.

Serve at room temperature.

Try This....
* Served with grilled sardines or any oily fish
* Alongside barbecued meat
* Simply spooned over wholegrain rice

See photograph on page 237.

Midlife Hack: Authentic dried terasi (also known as belacan) can be found in Asian supermarkets and needs to be fried before use. You can also buy shrimp paste in a jar, which is ready to use; just be sure to check the instructions before you embark.

Health Tip
Lemon grass, beyond having the most gorgeous aroma, has antibacterial and anti-inflammatory properties, which can help alleviate a range of health issues such as digestive disorders, infections and rheumatism.

WHY WE LOVE IT

A light, bright, pretty salsa, which will happily jazz up a simple piece of grilled fish. We love it with smoked mackerel, grilled sardines or pan-fried trout.

Radish, Cucumber & Herb Salsa

SERVES 4
MAKES APPROX. 200G

150g salad radishes, finely diced

¼ of a cucumber, finely diced

a handful of mint leaves, finely chopped

a handful of coriander leaves, finely chopped

1 spring onion, finely diced

juice of 1 lime

sea salt flakes and freshly ground black pepper

Combine all the ingredients in a bowl and serve.

Health Tip
Like other vegetables of the brassica family, radishes contain two natural compounds, sulforaphane and indole-3-carbinol, which are thought to have an anti-cancer action. Radishes also provide vitamin C to boost your defences against disease.

STRAWBERRY SALSA
WITH AVOCADO &
GREEN CHILLI

ZEHUG

MIDLIFE SALSA VERDE

RADISH, CUCUMBER
& HERB SALSA

SAMBAL MATAH

WHY WE LOVE IT

Who can resist anything with 'hug' in the name? This delicious, fresh relish is originally from Yemen and positively explodes with the flavours of the Middle East. It takes mere minutes to make, and promises to transform a simple piece of fish, chicken or meat into something really rather special.

Zehug

CORIANDER, CHILLI & TOMATO RELISH

SERVES 5–6
MAKES APPROX. 250–300G

2 cloves

5 cardamom pods, crushed

1 garlic clove, crushed

3 tbsp extra virgin olive oil

1 ripe tomato, diced

1 green chilli, finely diced, including seeds

a large handful of coriander leaves, roughly chopped

½ tsp ground cumin

½ tsp cumin seeds

sea salt flakes and freshly ground black pepper

Place the cloves and the seeds from the cardamom pods into a pestle and mortar and crush to release their aroma.

Tip the crushed seeds into a bowl, add the remaining ingredients and season. Mix well, then cover with clingfilm and leave to steep in the fridge for about 30 minutes before serving. It's best eaten immediately.

See photograph on page 237.

Midlife Hack: Deseeding cardamom pods means that you'll get a fresher flavour; simply smash the pods to release the black seeds within.

Health Tip
Studies have shown that fresh coriander leaves contain compounds that may be helpful in managing Alzheimer's disease due to their memory-improving and cholesterol-lowering properties.

WHY WE LOVE IT

The pairing of avocado and strawberries, with their antioxidant power, is complemented here by a hit of chilli and coriander. The result is a lively salsa that would be right at home at a summer BBQ.

MIND, MEMORY & MOOD

DIGESTIVE HEALTH

HEART HEALTH

BLOOD-SUGAR BALANCE

BONE & JOINT HEALTH

HORMONE HARMONY

SKIN, SENSES & IMMUNITY

ENERGY BOOSTING

Strawberry Salsa

WITH AVOCADO & GREEN CHILLI

SERVES 5–6
MAKES APPROX. 250–300G

150g strawberries, hulled, halved and sliced

1 ripe avocado, peeled, stoned and sliced

1 spring onion, finely chopped

a handful of coriander leaves, roughly chopped

1 green jalapeño chilli, deseeded and finely chopped

a pinch of sea salt flakes

freshly ground black pepper

Combine all the ingredients in a bowl and serve immediately.

See photograph on page 237.

Health Tip
Early studies indicate that strawberries may have the potential to provide benefits to the ageing brain.

WHY WE LOVE IT

For some reason we tend to eat red cabbage only at Christmas time, which is a shame because it really is delicious and versatile – as demonstrated by this cold, pickled version. There are masses of health benefits from the antioxidant-stacked red cabbage and red onion; the star anise and cardamom aid digestion, and our final Midlife masterstroke, apple cider vinegar, helps balance your blood sugar.

MIND, MEMORY & MOOD
DIGESTIVE HEALTH
HEART HEALTH
BLOOD-SUGAR BALANCE
BONE & JOINT HEALTH
HORMONE HARMONY
SKIN, SENSES & IMMUNITY
ENERGY BOOSTING

Spiced Red Cabbage Pickle

SERVES 6
MAKES APPROX. 750G

1 small head of red cabbage, thinly sliced

1 red onion, thinly sliced

50g raisins

50g dried cranberries

2 tbsp apple cider vinegar

2 star anise

5 cardamom pods, crushed

200ml water

sea salt flakes and freshly ground black pepper

Place all the ingredients in a large saucepan and bring to the boil, then reduce the heat and simmer gently for about 30 minutes until the onions and cabbage have softened and most of the liquid has evaporated (a little juice should remain for storage). Leave to cool, then chill before serving.

This keeps well in an airtight container in the fridge for up to 2 weeks.

Try This...
* Alongside barbecued pork
* With cheese and crackers
* As the basis for a salad, such as RGB Salad, see page 106

Health Tip
Red cabbage contains an impressive 36 anthocyanins; not all are easily absorbed, but with such an abundance of antioxidants, it's guaranteed to be good for you.

WHY WE LOVE IT

We discovered this fantastic relish on a trip to Peru, where so many health-food trends are emerging. At the Lima street-food stalls, it's made with the fragrant local aji chillies (plenty of them), and served alongside anything and everything. Aji are hard to find, so we've substituted jalapeño chillies – add more or less, depending on your appetite for heat. Salting and rinsing the red onions, then marinating them in lime juice, serves to sweeten and mellow them. The resulting relish is so good that Salsa Criolla is being hailed as 'the new ketchup' – which sounds about right to us.

MIND, MEMORY & MOOD

DIGESTIVE HEALTH

HEART HEALTH

BLOOD-SUGAR BALANCE

BONE & JOINT HEALTH

HORMONE HARMONY

SKIN, SENSES & IMMUNITY

ENERGY BOOSTING

Salsa Criolla

PERUVIAN RED ONION SALSA

SERVES 6
MAKES APPROX. 300G

1 large red onion, peeled

2 tsp sea salt flakes

1 aji chilli or jalapeño chilli, deseeded and sliced into very thin strips

a handful of mint, parsley or coriander leaves, thinly sliced

juice of 2 limes

1 strip of lime peel, very thinly sliced

1 tbsp cider vinegar

freshly ground black pepper

Health Tip

Red onions are particularly high in flavonoid antioxidants, the primary source of their pigmentation. One of them, quercetin, has been found to reduce blood pressure, the risk of stroke and coronary heart disease.

Slice the red onion very thinly using a sharp knife or mandoline – Peruvians call this 'a la pluma' (feather-like), so go as thin as you dare. Place in a bowl, add the salt and leave to stand for 10 minutes.

Rinse the onion well under cold running water and pat dry with kitchen paper, then put into a non-reactive bowl. Add the remaining ingredients and leave to marinate for 10 minutes before serving.

The salsa will keep in the fridge for 2 days.

Try This...

* Spooned over a hamburger or seared steak
* As a side for chilli con carne
* Served with Bliss Burgers, see page 146, or Green Egg Wraps, see page 180
* On crusty bread, or in a seeded tortilla wrap with hummus and tomatoes

Midlife Hack: It's the irritant chemical propanethial S-oxide in onions that triggers the tears. To limit the effect, chill onions before slicing and use a very sharp knife, which will cause less damage to cell walls, meaning fewer irritant compounds are released. Turn the 'cut' half towards the board as you slice.

WHY WE LOVE IT

If porridge and yogurt are your go-to breakfasts, as they are for us, then this 5-minute raw jam is an ingenious way to funk them up. A raw jam is simply fresh or frozen fruit blitzed with some cheeky chia seeds, which expand to provide the gelatinous quality that makes this a jam rather than a compote. You can use whatever soft fruit you have to hand, adding spices or herbs as the mood takes you – so be creative.

Raw Jam

MAKES APPROX. 300G

300g fresh or frozen soft fruit (defrosted) or a combination of fruits, such as hulled strawberries, raspberries, blueberries, blackberries, chopped mango or peeled kiwifruit

50ml water or coconut water

1 tsp lemon juice

2 tbsp chia seeds

1–2 tsp maple syrup, to taste (optional)

Put the fruit, water, lemon juice and chia seeds into a bowl and mash together. Alternatively, pulse in a food processor or blender to achieve a thick consistency. If the jam is too tart, stir in maple syrup to taste.

Chill in the fridge for at least 1 hour before serving to allow the chia seeds to thicken the jam and the flavours to develop. Store the jam in the fridge for up to 4 days.

Try This...
Some delicious raw jam flavour combinations:

* 300g mangoes, with 1 teaspoon of lime juice (replacing the lemon juice in the main recipe), 1/2 teaspoon of lime zest and 1/2 teaspoon of vanilla extract
* 300g blackberries and raspberries with black pepper and a little date syrup
* 300g strawberries and 1 tablespoon finely chopped mint leaves
* 300g blueberries and a pinch of mixed spice

Health Tip
Chia seeds are full of fibre, great for your digestion, and they can absorb up to ten times their weight in water – which is why they work so well to make raw jam.

WHY WE LOVE IT

Good old-fashioned apple sauce is a fantastic sweetener which has staged a comeback in the Midlife Kitchen. Eat it straight from the pot for an immediate sweet fix, spread it on a crêpe or stir it into porridge or yogurt (see Apple Strudel Yogurt on page 52). Date syrup will give you a rich, dark caramel colour, rather than the insipid pale-green of a shop-bought apple sauce.

MIND, MEMORY & MOOD · DIGESTIVE HEALTH · HEART HEALTH · BLOOD-SUGAR BALANCE · BONE & JOINT HEALTH · HORMONE HARMONY · SKIN, SENSES & IMMUNITY · ENERGY BOOSTING

Midlife Apple Sauce

MAKES APPROX. 500G

2 Bramley apples, about 500g in total, peeled, cored and roughly chopped

2 tbsp water

1 tsp ground cinnamon

2 cloves

2–3 tbsp Midlife Sweetener, see page 31, or 2 tbsp date syrup or maple syrup

Place all the ingredients in a saucepan and bring to a simmer, stirring. When the mixture begins to bubble, reduce the heat and cook gently, stirring occasionally, until the apples have disintegrated.

Remove the pan from the heat and give it a good stir to make a smooth sauce, or leave it chunkier if you prefer. Leave to cool, then chill. The sauce will keep in the fridge for up to a week.

Midlife Hack: This is easier still if you cook it in the microwave – just give it 2–3 minutes, covered, on full power. Make a batch, cool and then freeze in ice-cube trays; it defrosts in minutes for a quick breakfast bonus.

Health Tip
Apples really are nutritional superstars. In numerous epidemiological studies, they have been associated with a decreased risk of chronic diseases, such as cardiovascular disease, asthma and diabetes, due to their high antioxidant activity.

WHY WE LOVE IT

Our Caramel Sauce delivers all the unctuous gooeyness of a traditional toffee sauce, but (amazingly) with no butter at all, and coconut sugar replacing the usual caster. Of course, sugar is sugar whatever the form – and we all know that eating too much of it is no good thing; but coconut sugar does have a lower GI score than conventional table sugar, which means less of a blood-sugar spike when you do choose to indulge.

Caramel Sauce

SERVES 2

50g coconut sugar

a splash of water

50ml coconut milk

½ tsp vanilla extract

a pinch of sea salt flakes (optional)

Mix the coconut sugar with a splash of water in a small saucepan, then bring to a simmer. Add the coconut milk, vanilla and salt (if using); bring to a simmer and cook for 10 minutes, stirring occasionally, until the sauce is reduced and darkened.

Leave to cool slightly, then chill – it benefits from 30 minutes in the fridge to thicken before serving, but it can also be served warm. The sauce will keep in the fridge for up to a week.

Try This...
* With Midlife Sticky Toffee Puddings, see page 262
* Swirled into porridge
* As an alternative to date syrup to sweeten Apple Strudel Yogurt, see page 52

Health Tip
Coconut sugar tastes similar to brown sugar, but contains some nutrients and has a lower GI score. This sauce is slightly less sweet than conventional toffee sauces, but a spoonful still goes a long way...

GOOD
SWEET
STUFF

WHY WE LOVE IT

This gorgeous spiced syrup would work with any fruit you have to hand, but we love it with a combination of delicate white and pale-green exotic fruit. The crushed coriander seeds are a revelation, bringing an aromatic burst to every bite. The xylitol is an experiment for us; we're always keen to find natural sugar substitutes that deliver sweetness without a chemical aftertaste, and here we think it works really well. If in doubt, substitute a light clear honey, such as acacia.

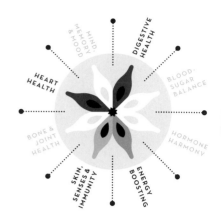

White Fruit Salad
WITH CORIANDER SEED & LIME SYRUP

SERVES 4

1 nashi pear

1 apple

1/2 a white dragon fruit, peeled

2 mangosteen, peeled and segmented

10 fresh or canned lychees

10 white seedless grapes

FOR THE SYRUP

juice of 2 limes

2 tbsp xylitol or runny acacia honey

2 tsp coriander seeds, crushed

2 cloves

a grind of vanilla bean, see page 211, or the seeds from a pod

Place all the syrup ingredients in a small saucepan, bring to a simmer and cook for 5 minutes until reduced and slightly thickened. Leave to cool, then chill in the fridge.

Peel, quarter and core the pear and apple, then cut all the fruit into bite-sized pieces and place in serving bowls. Dress liberally with the fragrant chilled syrup and serve.

Midlife Hack: Some of the fruits we use can be tricky to find, so substitute fruits of your choice – for example, white melon or pear.

Health Tip
Xylitol is a natural substance extracted from corn cobs or birch bark – it has the same sweetness as sugar, but 40 per cent fewer calories, a lower GI and it won't damage your teeth. It even feeds friendly microbes in the gut.

WHY WE LOVE IT

Most of the fruit salad ingredients are store-cupboard items that, with the addition of ricotta and oranges, can be transformed into this delicious, decadent dessert in a matter of minutes. It's a grown-up mouthful – not overly sweet, richly spiced and darkly aromatic, like Christmas in a bowl.

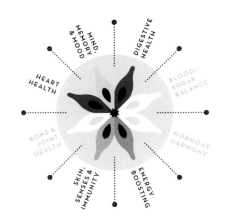

Warm Winter Fruit Salad

WITH ORANGE RICOTTA

SERVES 4–6

80g soft dried apricots

80g soft dried figs

60g soft prunes

60g dried pears

60g dried cherries

30g dried cranberries

60g ready-cooked and peeled chestnuts from a packet

300ml Earl Grey tea

juice of 1 orange

2 strips of orange peel, each about 7cm long

1 cinnamon stick, broken in 2

2 star anise

FOR THE ORANGE RICOTTA

100g ricotta cheese

2 tsp orange zest

1 tbsp fresh orange juice

Place all the fruit salad ingredients in a large saucepan, bring to a simmer and cook, uncovered, for 10 minutes until the fruit has plumped up. Remove the fruit from the pan and set aside.

Return the pan to the heat and simmer the liquid for a further 5 minutes until reduced, then pour over the fruit and leave to cool.

Meanwhile, combine all the orange ricotta ingredients in a bowl.

Serve the warm fruit salad with the orange ricotta on the side.

Midlife Hack: Remove the star anise and cinnamon stick and pulse the cooled fruit in a food processor or blender to make a gorgeous healthy marmalade to stir into your morning yogurt, or a great chutney to serve alongside a good strong Cheddar.

Health Tip
Dried fruit is nutrient dense and a convenient source of fibre, excellent for digestive health.

WHY WE LOVE IT

Simple, fresh, healthy and interesting – you'll know by now that these are our watchwords in the Midlife Kitchen, and this ingenious idea is all of those things. Include anything from your fruit bowl and experiment – the spring rolls are great pepped up with a hint of finely sliced chilli, or with soft herbs such as mint or basil. Nuts, seeds and dried fruit add another dimension.

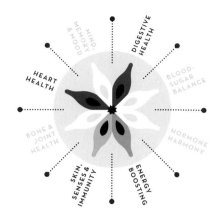

Fresh Fruit Spring Rolls

MAKES 6 ROLLS

FOR THE ROLLS

2 or 3 strawberries, sliced

½ kiwifruit, peeled and sliced

½ banana, peeled and sliced

a few pieces of pineapple, chopped

a few pieces of mango, chopped

6 rice paper wrappers

warm water

a few mint leaves, finely sliced

6 walnut halves, chopped

3 Medjool dates, pitted and chopped

2 tsp desiccated coconut

1 tsp finely grated lime zest

FOR THE DIPPING SAUCE

juice of 3 limes

1 tbsp runny honey, maple syrup or date syrup

1 star anise

Combine all the dipping sauce ingredients in a small bowl and set aside.

Pat the prepared fruit dry with kitchen paper to prevent the rolls becoming too slippery.

Lay a rice paper wrapper on a chopping board. Using a pastry brush, moisten the sheet lightly with warm water so that it softens. Place some of the fruit on the top third or so of the wrapper and scatter with your choice of the remaining ingredients (our 3 favourite combos are mango, pineapple, desiccated coconut and lime zest; strawberry, kiwi and mint; banana, walnut and date).

Taking the top edge of the wrapper, fold it down over the filling. Fold the edges in from the left and right and keep rolling up, tucking in the edges as you go, as if you are wrapping a present. It takes a little practice, but aim to create a fairly tight cylinder. Repeat with the remaining ingredients to make 6 rolls.

Serve immediately, doused with plenty of dipping sauce.

Health Tip
The NHS recommends that we eat five 80g portions of a variety of fruit and vegetables every day as they are an excellent source of vitamins, minerals and fibre. These fresh fruit rolls are a delicious way to do it.

WHY WE LOVE IT

This is a glorious pot of plummy flavour and nutty crunch. The secret to a good crumble is a really crisp topping – guaranteed with our Midlife Grown-up Granola, which doesn't just deliver crunch and speed, but is also full of stealth health from the Brazils, almonds, cashews, oats and amaranth. Serve with warm plum juice for an autumn treat.

Elderflower & Granola Plumble

SERVES 2

350g fresh or frozen plums or damsons, halved and stoned

1 tbsp elderflower cordial

1 tbsp maple syrup

a grind of vanilla bean, see page 211, or the seeds from a pod

4–6 tbsp Midlife Grown-up Granola, see page 29

1 tbsp coconut flakes (optional)

2 tsp demerara sugar (optional)

Preheat the oven to 180°C/Gas Mark 4.

Place the plums or damsons in a saucepan, add the elderflower cordial, maple syrup and vanilla, bring to a simmer and cook for 5 minutes until the plums are just beginning to soften.

Use a slotted spoon to divide the warm plums between 2 ramekins or a small copper pan (pictured), leaving any extra juice to serve on the side. The plums should be moist, but not swimming in liquid.

Cover the fruit with the granola and sprinkle with the coconut flakes and sugar, if using.

Bake for 15 minutes until the tops are golden brown, toasty and crunchy, and the fruit is bubbling through. Serve with the reserved juice on the side.

Health Tip
Thanks to their high vitamin C content, plums fortify the immune system (useful, as autumn chills generally arrive at the same time as the plum glut). Vit C will also assist iron absorption in the body, which helps boost energy as the days get shorter.

WHY WE LOVE IT

This delicate dessert makes a lovely light end to a meal. The tender pears sit prettily in a honeyed syrup, with ginger and cardamom lending a warm bass-note buzz. Add a drizzle of melted dark chocolate for a more indulgent pud.

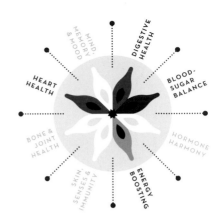

Drenched Cardamom & Ginger Pears

WITH AMARETTI & ALMOND CRUMB

SERVES 4

750ml perry or cider

6 cardamom pods, crushed

a thumb-sized piece of fresh root ginger, peeled and sliced

1 cinnamon stick, broken in half

1 strip of lemon peel, about 6cm long

2 tbsp runny acacia honey

4 firm but just ripe Comice or Williams pears

a squeeze of lemon juice

TO SERVE

50g dark chocolate, melted (optional)

a handful of almonds, with skins on, thinly sliced

2 Amaretti biscuits, crushed

Put the perry or cider, cardamom, ginger, cinnamon stick, lemon peel and honey into a deep, lidded saucepan and bring to the boil, then reduce the heat and simmer for 5–10 minutes, stirring occasionally.

Meanwhile, peel the pears, leaving the stalks intact, then squeeze with a little lemon juice to prevent discolouration.

Lay the pears on their sides in the poaching liquid, cover with a lid and simmer for 20–30 minutes (the timing will depend on the pear variety and ripeness), turning occasionally, until evenly poached and softened. The thickest part of each pear should be tender when pierced with a sharp knife. Remove the pears from the pan, place in a bowl and leave to cool, then transfer to the fridge.

Return the pan to the heat and bring the poaching liquid to a strong simmer and cook for 10 minutes until reduced by about half. Pour the syrup over the pears and leave to cool, then chill in the fridge for an hour or more.

When ready to serve the pears, add a drizzle of melted dark chocolate (if using), and scatter with almond slivers and crushed Amaretti.

Health Tip
In addition to dispensing a good dose of antioxidants and potassium, pears contain soluble fibre (pectin), known to improve digestion, lower cholesterol levels and help moderate blood sugar.

WHY WE LOVE IT

'Blueberries Improve Memory in Older Adults' – it's a stark headline, and well worth remembering next time you're planning what's for dessert. A fruit soup sounds oddly anachronistic, but a Blueberry Gazpacho? Irresistible. A garnish of black pepper really does work – give it a go – while edible flowers are gorgeously pointless. Never underestimate the power of pretty.

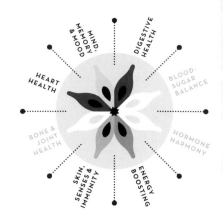

Blueberry Gazpacho

SERVES 4

300g fresh or frozen blueberries

200g fresh or frozen raspberries

3 tbsp date syrup

a splash of water

juice of 2 oranges

grated zest of 1 orange

1 tbsp lemon juice

a grind of vanilla bean, see page 211, or the seeds from a pod

TO SERVE (OPTIONAL)

freshly ground black pepper

edible flowers

Place half the berries in a saucepan with the date syrup and a splash of water, bring to a simmer and cook for 3 minutes until the berries burst and release their juices. Remove from the heat, leave to cool, then chill.

Put the remaining berries into a food processor or blender with the orange juice and zest, lemon juice and vanilla. Blitz until smooth, then combine with the chilled cooked berries.

Chill again, then serve with a grind of black pepper and edible flowers.

Midlife Hack: For a sensational sorbet, freeze this gazpacho mix, stirring occasionally with a fork to break up the ice crystals. Strawberries and blackcurrants work well in this gazpacho too.

Health Tip
A 2009 study found that cooking blueberries for a short burst, as we do here, increases antioxidant activity, probably because it breaks down cell walls.

WHY WE LOVE IT

Who doesn't love cheesecake? Sam loves it so much that she had one as her wedding cake, so it was a top priority for us to devise a healthier way to enjoy this divine dessert. Our version is lightened with ricotta and yogurt and underpinned by a nutty base – with pumpkin purée, fresh ginger and cinnamon as the Midlife trump cards. The result is a rather spectacular and wholesome centrepiece, great for any get-together.

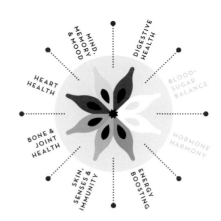

Pumpkin & Ginger Cheesecake

WITH HONEY & FRESH RASPBERRIES

SERVES 8

125g Midlife LSA, see page 27, or ground almonds

2 tsp ground ginger

75g Medjool dates, pitted and finely chopped

2 tbsp coconut oil, melted if solid

1 egg white, lightly whisked

a handful of fresh raspberries, to serve

FOR THE FILLING

250g ricotta cheese

150g thick Greek yogurt

400g can pumpkin purée (100 per cent pumpkin)

60ml runny honey, plus extra to serve

2 large eggs

2 tbsp lemon juice

2 tsp ground cinnamon

1 tbsp peeled and finely grated fresh root ginger

Preheat the oven to 180°C/Gas Mark 4. Line a 20cm springform cake tin with greaseproof paper.

To make the base, combine the LSA or ground almonds, ground ginger, dates and coconut oil in a bowl. Mix well, using your fingers to create a crumb, ensuring the dates are evenly distributed. Press the mixture firmly into the bottom of the prepared tin, then brush it with egg white (this keeps the base layer crisp) and bake for 10 minutes. Remove from the oven and leave to cool completely.

Reduce the oven temperature to 160°C/Gas Mark 3.

To make the filling, put the ricotta cheese into a food processor or blender and whizz until completely smooth. Add the remaining filling ingredients and blend until combined.

Pour the filling over the cooled base, then bake for 50 minutes until the cheesecake is cooked through but still has a bit of a wobble in the middle. Turn off the oven, leaving the cake inside to cool completely. Transfer to the fridge and chill for at least 2 hours to firm up.

To serve, remove the cheesecake from the tin, place on a serving dish and top with the raspberries. Drizzle with honey just before serving. This cheesecake is deliberately not overly sweet so, for those with a sweeter tooth, serve with a little extra honey on the side.

Health Tip
Pumpkin has been shown in studies to have an anti-diabetic effect, which means it can help stabilize and control blood-glucose levels.

WHY WE LOVE IT

A 10-minute mini marvel, these little puddings are completely fat-free, with the sweetness coming from our favourite Medjool dates. You get a real lift from the whisked egg white, resulting in a very light but wonderfully sticky mouthful.

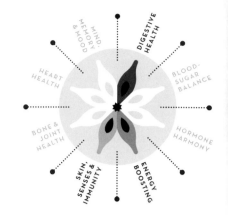

Midlife Sticky Toffee Puddings

SERVES 4

175g Medjool dates, pitted

175ml water

2 tbsp maple syrup

1 tsp vanilla extract

2 large eggs, separated

85g self-raising flour

a pinch of sea salt flakes

1 tsp bicarbonate of soda

4 tbsp date syrup

Health Tip
A recent study found that date syrup shows promise for fighting bacterial infections, and dates are a good source of gut-friendly fibre too.

Preheat the oven to 160°C/Gas Mark 3.

Place the dates and water in a saucepan and bring to a simmer, then cook for 3–4 minutes until softened. Leave to cool slightly, then transfer to a food processor or blender, add the maple syrup and vanilla extract and blitz until almost smooth. Tip into a bowl and stir in the egg yolks. Sift in the flour, add the salt and bicarbonate of soda and stir well.

Whisk the egg whites in a clean bowl until stiff peaks form, then fold into the date mixture, ensuring they are fully incorporated.

Put 1 tablespoon of the date syrup into each of 4 pudding moulds or ramekins, then divide the mixture between them. Transfer the moulds to a roasting tin and pour hot water into the tin to reach halfway up the moulds.

Bake for 25–30 minutes, or until a skewer inserted into the puddings comes out clean (the timing will depend on the depth of the moulds or ramekins). Run a knife around the edge of the moulds, then invert the puddings on to individual plates. Serve immediately.

These puddings don't require any extra sweetness, but if you're keen to add a sauce, try our Caramel Sauce (pictured), see page 245.

WHY WE LOVE IT

This is the kind of pudding to serve straight from oven to table, so that picky fingers can get at the sticky edges as a stand-in for seconds. It's a take on a crumble, of course – but this streusel version is made in a shallow dish with the topping in clusters, delivering a crisp crunch over a layer of oozy black fruit, which manages the clever Midlife trick of being both healthy and opulent in equal measure. Our Power Porridge mix brings LSA and oat bran to the table, nuts and seeds add their health dividend, and date syrup stands in for much of the sugar in a conventional crumble topping.

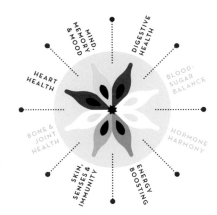

Black & Blue Berry Streusel

SERVES 8

100g butter, melted

75g Midlife Power Porridge, see page 28, or jumbo oats

40g flaked almonds

30g sunflower seeds

70g wholemeal flour

1 tsp ground cinnamon

50g soft light brown sugar

3 tbsp date syrup

300g fresh or frozen blackberries

200g fresh or frozen blueberries

Preheat the oven to 180°C/Gas Mark 4.

For the streusel topping, mix all the ingredients, except the berries, in a large bowl.

Place the berries in a single layer in a shallow baking dish and scatter with the topping. Place it in clusters rather than trying to cover all of the fruit, to form a patchwork of streusel and berries.

Bake for 20–25 minutes until the fruit is sticky and bubbling and the topping is crisp.

Midlife Hack: You can make this with fresh or frozen fruit; if you're raiding the freezer, a handful of frozen black cherries, black plums or blackcurrants could easily be added to bump up the berry bonanza.

Health Tip
Blackberries, like all dark berries, are among the healthiest fruit, thanks to their plant pigments. A study for the American Cancer Society found that those who eat the most berries are significantly less likely to die from cardiovascular disease.

WHY WE LOVE IT

Deliciously decadent, and not a drop of double cream in sight!
This quickie mousse uses natural yogurt for its voluptuous
creaminess, and whisked egg whites for lift. Yes, there's some
sugar – use 3 tablespoons if you prefer a truly dark spoonful,
or 4 if you have a sweet tooth. Do serve in small bowls or glasses,
though; this is surprisingly rich and indulgent and will easily satisfy
six chocoholics.

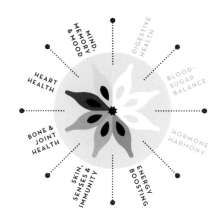

Five-minute Chocolate Mousse

SERVES 6

200g dark chocolate
(70% cocoa solids),
broken into pieces

4 egg whites

3–4 tbsp caster sugar, to taste

150g natural yogurt

fresh raspberries, to serve

Melt the chocolate in a heatproof bowl set over a saucepan
of gently simmering water, making sure the bowl does not
touch the water, stirring occasionally. Alternatively, melt
the chocolate in a microwave. Leave to cool slightly.

Meanwhile, whisk the egg whites in a clean bowl until stiff
peaks form. Gently fold in the sugar, a spoonful at a time.

Mix the yogurt into the melted chocolate (it will start to
thicken immediately, so work fairly quickly), then fold in the
egg white mixture, a third at a time.

Spoon the mousse into 6 small bowls or glasses and serve
immediately or chill to serve later (we give you 5 minutes!).
Serve with fresh raspberries and small spoons.

Health Tip
According to a study by the
University of Copenhagen, dark
chocolate is far more satisfying
than milk chocolate, lessening
our cravings for sweet, salty
and fatty foods.

WHY WE LOVE IT

Let's face it, there are times when only cake will do. But not all cakes are created equal; with a bit of Midlife manipulation, they can be a healthy indulgence, particularly when the quantity of sugar and flour is limited and the main ingredients are, instead, yogurt, olive oil and almonds. This moist, golden cake works well as a dessert, served warm with a dollop of yogurt, slivers of almond and fresh orange segments.

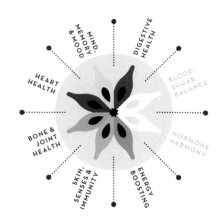

Yogurt, Almond & Orange Drizzle Cake

MAKES 8 SMALL CAKES OR 1 LARGE CAKE

150g natural yogurt

150g ground almonds

150g self-raising flour

75g soft brown sugar

100ml olive oil

3 eggs

1 tsp vanilla extract

1 tbsp clear honey

1 tsp saffron threads, soaked in 1 tsp boiling water

grated zest of 1 orange

2 tsp baking powder

a pinch of sea salt flakes

a grating of nutmeg

FOR THE SYRUP

juice of 2 oranges

1 tbsp runny honey

Preheat the oven to 170°C/Gas Mark 3½. Line an 8-hole mini loaf tin with individual cases, or use a nonstick liner in a 450g loaf tin.

Combine all the ingredients either using a stand mixer or hand-held mixer and beat well to form a smooth batter. Pour the mixture into the prepared tin and bake for 30 minutes for small cases or 40–45 minutes for a large loaf, until firm and golden and a skewer inserted into the centre comes out clean.

To make the syrup, heat the orange juice and honey in a small saucepan over a low heat.

Remove the cake or cakes from the oven, pierce a few times with a skewer and drizzle with the honey syrup. Leave to cool in the tin. Serve warm or at room temperature, with a spoonful of yogurt, almond slivers or fresh orange segments.

Try This...
Replace the saffron, orange zest and nutmeg with:

* the grated zest of 1 lemon, 1 teaspoon of poppy seeds and drizzle with a lemon and honey syrup
* 2 tablespoons crushed pistachios, the zest of 1 lime, a grind of vanilla bean, or the seeds from a vanilla pod, and drizzle with a lime and honey syrup

Midlife Hack: If you are gluten intolerant, this cake works with 300g ground almonds – you'll just get a denser crumb.

Health Tip
Swapping half of the flour in a regular cake recipe for ground almonds doesn't just bring flavour and texture: there's protein in those nutritious little nuts, plus vitamin E and magnesium.

WHY WE LOVE IT

The perfect antidote to those pale and sugary fairy cakes that make your teeth ache, this devilishly dark ginger cake packs a real punch, thanks to its mighty trio of gingers: ground, fresh and stem. A slick of black treacle and warming spices add more depth, and, while the hint of chilli is optional, it's well worth adding if you like a full-on flavour sensation. The upshot is a very grown-up cake, best eaten in small, sticky, sumptuous squares – perhaps on a cold day with a strong cup of tea and a smile on your face.

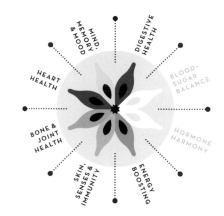

MIND, MEMORY & MOOD · DIGESTIVE HEALTH · BLOOD-SUGAR BALANCE · HEART HEALTH · HORMONE HARMONY · BONE & JOINT HEALTH · ENERGY BOOSTING · SKIN, SENSES & IMMUNITY

Three-ginger Fire Cake

MAKES ABOUT 16 SQUARES

50g butter

100g black treacle

100g date syrup

80g dark muscovado sugar

60ml milk

60g stem ginger, roughly chopped

1 egg, beaten

2 tsp peeled and grated fresh root ginger

200g self-raising flour

5 tsp ground ginger

1 tsp ground cinnamon

1 tsp allspice

1 tsp chilli powder, or less to taste (optional)

a pinch of sea salt flakes

1 tsp bicarbonate of soda

2 tbsp stem ginger syrup (from the stem ginger jar)

Preheat the oven to 160°C/Gas Mark 3. Line a baking tin, about 30 x 30cm, with nonstick baking paper.

Place the butter, treacle, syrup and sugar in a large saucepan and melt over a medium heat, stirring gently to combine. Remove the pan from the heat and leave to cool slightly.

Add the milk and stem ginger, then stir in the beaten egg and root ginger. Sift all the dry ingredients into the mixture and combine.

Spoon the mixture into the prepared tin and bake for 30–35 minutes until cooked through and a skewer inserted in the centre comes out clean. While still warm and in the tin, prick the cake a dozen times with a skewer, then spoon the stem ginger syrup over the top. Leave to cool.

Cut into 16 smallish squares to serve. Store in an airtight container for up to a week.

Health Tip
Gingerol, the main bioactive compound in ginger, is known to have powerful immunity-boosting, anti-inflammatory and antioxidant effects, which can be helpful for sufferers of osteoarthritis.

WHY WE LOVE IT

This book is, of course, devoted to healthy eating in midlife, with the explicit aim of living longer... But we reckon there's little point living longer if there's no cake in your life. So, one of our prime preoccupations at the Midlife Kitchen has been to develop cake recipes that taste truly scrumptious, but don't serve up a mouthful of guilt with every bite. This moist cake easily made the cut: familiar, comforting and tasty, but we've kept the butter and sugar quota to a minimum, while the introduction of apples, cranberries and spicing brings a happy health hit to teatime.

Spiced Apple & Cranberry Cake

MAKES A 20CM CAKE

200g self-raising flour

2 tsp ground cinnamon

a grating of nutmeg

a grind of vanilla bean, see page 211, or the seeds from a pod

1 tsp baking powder

a pinch of sea salt flakes

100g cold butter, diced

100g soft light brown sugar

2 eggs, beaten

125ml milk

½ tsp vanilla extract

225g Bramley apples, peeled, cored and roughly diced into 2cm cubes

80g dried cranberries

2 tbsp sunflower seeds

1 tsp demerara sugar

Midlife Apple Sauce, see page 244, to serve (optional)

Health Tip
Apples are, as we all know, super shots of fibre – but they also contain numerous potent phytochemicals, including quercetin and catechins, which studies have found can play a key role in reducing chronic disease risk, particularly cardiovascular disease, asthma and type 2 diabetes.

Preheat the oven to 160°C/Gas Mark 3. Line a 20cm diameter springform cake tin with nonstick baking paper.

Place the flour, cinnamon, nutmeg, grind of vanilla bean, baking powder and salt in a food processor. Add the diced butter and pulse until the mixture resembles fine breadcrumbs. Add the soft brown sugar and pulse again.

Whisk the eggs, milk and vanilla extract in a jug, then pour into the processor and pulse to form a smooth, thick batter. Add the chopped apples to the batter with the cranberries and stir to combine (without breaking down the apples too much).

Spoon the mixture into the prepared tin and scatter with the sunflower seeds and demerara sugar. Bake for 40 minutes until golden brown and a skewer inserted in the centre comes out clean.

Leave to cool in the tin for a few minutes, then transfer to a wire rack. Serve warm or at room temperature, perhaps with Midlife Apple Sauce on the side. Store in an airtight container for up to 3 days.

Midlife Hack: Add a handful of frozen cranberries to the Midlife Apple Sauce recipe for a tart, pink, pretty accompaniment to this cake.

WHY WE LOVE IT

We're quite partial to a slice of carrot cake – but our enjoyment is always tempered by the knowledge that there's nothing particularly healthy about it (apart from the word 'carrot' in the title). So, we set ourselves the task of coming up with a truly healthy carrot cake for the Midlife Kitchen: all the magic of the cake, but with the nutritional value bumped up, the sat fats reduced and portion control built in. Using Midlife Power Porridge brings our nutty LSA into the mix, while the oats, carrots, walnuts and cinnamon keep these heavenly chewy cookies on the right side of virtuous.

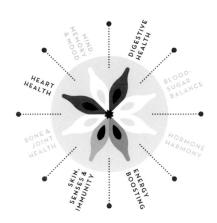

Carrot Cake Bites

MAKES 15–20

100g Midlife Power Porridge, see page 28, or jumbo oats

80g wholemeal flour

1 tsp bicarbonate of soda

1 heaped tsp ground cinnamon

a pinch of sea salt flakes

50g butter, melted

1 egg

1 tsp vanilla extract

75ml maple syrup or date syrup

100g carrots, peeled and roughly grated

50g sultanas

50g walnuts, chopped

chopped pecan nuts, to serve

FOR THE DRIZZLE

25g cream cheese

1 tbsp lemon juice

1 tbsp maple syrup

Health Tip
Lutein, one of the most common antioxidants in carrots, is important for eye health, while their plentiful carotenoids have been linked to improved immune function and reduced risk of degenerative disease.

Combine the oats, flour, bicarbonate of soda, cinnamon and salt in a bowl. In a separate bowl, mix the melted butter, egg, vanilla extract and maple or date syrup, then stir in the carrots, sultanas and walnuts. Add the carrot mix to the flour and oats, stirring well to combine. Chill for 30 minutes.

Preheat the oven to 180°C/Gas Mark 4. Line a baking sheet with nonstick baking paper.

Spoon 15–20 heaped tablespoons of the dough on to the baking sheet, fairly well spaced, then flatten slightly with the spoon. Chill again for 5 minutes.

Bake for 12–15 minutes until the cookies are crisp and golden on the outside. Leave to cool slightly on the sheet, then transfer to a wire rack to cool completely.

To make the drizzle topping, combine the cream cheese, lemon juice and maple syrup in a bowl and stir well until smooth. Using a teaspoon, gently drizzle a little over each cooled cookie and top with a scattering of chopped pecan nuts.

The cookies can be stored in an airtight container for up to 3 days.

Try This...
* For a more indulgent frosting to use in place of the drizzle topping, mix 50g cream cheese, 25g softened butter and 2 tablespoons of icing sugar in a bowl, beating with a spoon until smooth. Smear the frosting on to each cooled cookie

WHY WE LOVE IT

A truly healthy cake is, we've found, a rare treasure – very often, the taste or texture is all wrong because the usual delicious alchemy of fats and sugars has been lost in translation. We put our minds to creating something that really works and tastes divine, and here it is: a Midlife marvel in a loaf tin, bursting with flavour, low on fat and with just the right amount of squidge. Perfect with afternoon tea.

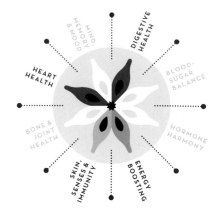

Teatime Walnut & Banana Loaf

MAKES 1 LOAF

40g butter, softened

150g wholemeal flour, plus extra for dusting

100g date sugar or soft light brown sugar

1 large egg

100ml milk

2½ tsp baking powder

2 tsp mixed spice

2 ripe bananas, roughly mashed

30g walnuts, chopped

30g pitted dates, chopped

Preheat the oven to 170°C/Gas Mark 3½. Line a 450g loaf tin.

Using a hand-held or stand mixer, cream the butter and sugar, then beat in the egg and milk. Sift in the flour, baking powder and mixed spice, then use a metal spoon to fold in until incorporated. Add the bananas, walnuts and dates and stir again.

Pour the batter into the prepared tin and bake for 1 hour or until a skewer inserted into the centre comes out clean. Leave to cool slightly in the tin, then turn out on to a wire rack. The cake is best served warm.

Midlife Hack: Date sugar is well worth seeking out as an alternative to regular sugar if you bake a lot. It's available from online retailers.

Health Tip
Date sugar came top in a study ranking 12 of the most popular sweeteners by their antioxidant content – not that surprising, as date sugar is simply whole, dried dates pulverized into a powder.

FIG, WALNUT & GINGER
UNCOOKIES

RAISIN, COCONUT
& CINNAMON
UNCOOKIES

DATE, APRICOT
& CARDAMOM
UNCOOKIES

CHOCOLATE, ORANGE
& BRAZIL NUT
UNCOOKIES

WHY WE LOVE IT

We like the idea of an 'energy ball', a healthy way to get a sweet fix without too much refined sugar. This is our Midlife version: the delicious, nutritious little 'uncookie' – perfect for those 'I need something now' moments (usually around mid-afternoon or after an exercise class), they go impressively well with a shot of espresso.

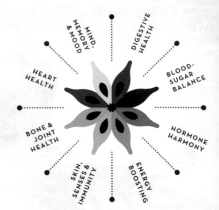

Uncookies

Health Tip
Don't be put off nuts because they are relatively high in calories – they're full of protein and fibre to keep you feeling full, so you'll probably eat less overall. Studies have shown that people who consume nuts are less likely to be overweight than those who don't.

Put all the ingredients, except the coatings, into a food processor and whizz, scraping down the sides between pulses using a spatula if necessary, until the ingredients are fully incorporated and the 'dough' is as chunky or as smooth as you like (we prefer it a little chunky). If the mixture is too dry, add more water; if too wet, add more LSA or ground almonds – it should be soft but not too sticky.

Take a heaped teaspoon of the mixture and form into small cookie shapes, about 3–4cm each in diameter, then coat with the coating ingredients. Chill for about 15 minutes to firm them up – this makes them deliciously chewy.

They will keep in the fridge in an airtight container for up to a week, but we can assure you that they won't hang around that long!

See photograph on pages 278–9.

FIG, WALNUT & GINGER

MAKES 10–12

2 tbsp Midlife LSA, see page 27, or ground almonds

200g soft dried figs

2 tbsp cold water

juice of 1 lime

50g walnuts, crushed

1 tsp peeled and finely grated fresh root ginger

1 tsp ground cinnamon

a pinch of sea salt flakes

FOR THE COATING

2 tbsp Midlife LSA, see page 27, or ground almonds

CHOCOLATE, ORANGE & BRAZIL NUT

MAKES 10–12

200g Medjool dates, pitted

2 tbsp freshly squeezed orange juice

1 tsp orange zest

6 Brazil nuts, finely chopped

2 tbsp Midlife LSA, see page 27, or ground almonds

a pinch of sea salt flakes

FOR THE COATING

2 tbsp unsweetened cocoa powder

RAISIN, COCONUT & CINNAMON

MAKES 10–12

2 tbsp desiccated coconut

150g raisins

2 tbsp cold water

a squeeze of lemon juice

2 tbsp almond butter

3 tbsp Midlife LSA, see page 27, or ground almonds

1 tsp ground cinnamon

FOR THE COATING

2 tbsp desiccated coconut

DATE, APRICOT & CARDAMOM

MAKES 10–12

10–15 cardamom pods, to taste

150g Medjool dates, pitted

50g dried apricots, chopped

2–3 tbsp water

finely grated zest of 1 lemon

3 tbsp Midlife LSA, see page 27, or ground almonds

2 tbsp desiccated coconut

FOR THE COATING

2 tbsp pistachio nuts, finely crushed

DRINKS

WHY WE LOVE IT

A refreshing and uplifting wake-up infusion; we've kept it super simple, because nobody wants to be messing around with heaps of ingredients first thing in the morning, and the honey is optional if you prefer a sugar-free start to the day.

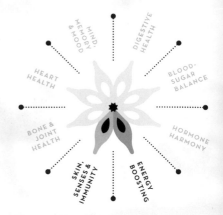

MIND, MEMORY & MOOD

DIGESTIVE HEALTH

HEART HEALTH

BLOOD-SUGAR BALANCE

BONE & JOINT HEALTH

HORMONE HARMONY

SKIN, SENSES & IMMUNITY

ENERGY BOOSTING

Sunrise Tea

SERVES 1

2 lemon grass stalks

a small handful of mint leaves

1 tsp runny honey

Bruise the lemon grass with a rolling pin and place in a mug. Add the mint and honey, then add boiling water.

Steep for 5 minutes, stirring with the lemon grass stalks.

Midlife Hack: Lemon grass stalks are hollow inside so they make great natural drinking straws.

Health Tip
The menthol component that gives mint its distinctive aroma stimulates the hippocampus area of the brain, which controls mental clarity and memory. Just the job first thing!

WHY WE LOVE IT

A refresher course of healthy vits, minerals and antioxidants, this hydrating tonic is a real eye-opener – who knew that simple celery could have so many health benefits? We love the delicate pale green combo of celery, cucumber and apple – all you need to do is gather them together and blitz away.

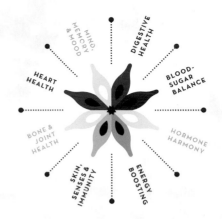

Wake-up Tonic

SERVES 2

½ a cucumber, peeled and roughly chopped

2 celery sticks, tougher strings removed, roughly chopped

1 apple, peeled, quartered and cored

juice of 1 lime

300ml chilled coconut water

Put all the ingredients into a blender and blitz well, then pour into 2 glasses and serve immediately (it will separate if left to stand).

Midlife Hack: The Midlife Kitchen requires little in the way of specialist cooking equipment – but we do love our NutriBullet 'extractors' because they can pulverize most fruit and veg without peeling or coring, which means more nutritional value, more fibre… and a lot less washing up.

Health Tip

Celery is a great antioxidant and anti-inflammatory, and it provides plenty of fibre too. It can help regulate blood pressure, thanks to its potassium content, while coumarin, an antioxidant found in celery, has been found to enhance the activity of white blood cells.

WHY WE LOVE IT

Jamu is an intrinsic part of Balinese life, a daily ritual to ward off ill health, thanks to the amazing antibacterial and anti-inflammatory properties of its key ingredient, turmeric. It's something of an acquired taste, so to make it more approachable we've added the familiar citrus tang of lime and orange juice, which also boosts the vitamin C content, making this an immunity-boosting Midlife Elixir.

MIND, MEMORY & MOOD
DIGESTIVE HEALTH
HEART HEALTH
BLOOD-SUGAR BALANCE
BONE & JOINT HEALTH
HORMONE HARMONY
SKIN, SENSES & IMMUNITY
ENERGY BOOSTING

Jamu

INDONESIAN TURMERIC JUICE

SERVES 2

50g fresh turmeric root, peeled and sliced

25g fresh root ginger, peeled and sliced

juice of 1 lime

juice of 1 orange

150ml chilled coconut water

1 tsp runny honey

sea salt flakes and freshly ground black pepper

ice cubes, to serve (optional)

Put all the ingredients into a blender with a small pinch of sea salt flakes and a grind of pepper, then blitz for 1 minute.

Strain the juice through a fine sieve or tea strainer into 2 glasses and serve, over ice if you prefer.

Midlife Hack: It's a good idea to use clingfilm as a barrier between your fingers and the turmeric when peeling and slicing as the staining can be difficult to remove.

Health Tip
Studies show that the curcumin found in turmeric may help fight infections and some cancers, reduce inflammation and treat digestive problems. The addition of black pepper, which contains piperine, increases the body's ability to absorb the curcumin.

WHY WE LOVE IT

A thick shake may not sound massively healthy, and that's exactly why we had such fun with this recipe. It tastes super indulgent, but every ingredient is happily working wonders: bananas for potassium and energy, avocado for good fats and cinnamon for antioxidant protection.

MIND, MEMORY & MOOD

DIGESTIVE HEALTH

HEART HEALTH

BLOOD-SUGAR BALANCE

BONE & JOINT HEALTH

HORMONE HARMONY

SKIN, SENSES & IMMUNITY

ENERGY BOOSTING

Bananacado Thick Shake

SERVES 1–2

1 banana, peeled, chopped and frozen

1/2 a ripe avocado, chopped

100ml semi-skimmed milk or unsweetened almond milk, see page 296

1/2 tsp ground cinnamon

Put all the ingredients into a blender and blend well for 1–2 minutes until the banana is completely incorporated.

Pour into 1 large or 2 smaller glasses and serve immediately.

Midlife Hack: If you have bananas that are past their best, just peel and freeze them, ready for shakes and smoothies.

Health Tip
Bananas are not only cheap and readily available, they are also an excellent energy source during exercise.

WHY WE LOVE IT

This dark, delicious juice looks – and tastes – deeply indulgent, yet takes mere minutes to make. You'll get a hit of vital minerals from the beetroot, powerful phytonutrients from the berries, plus a spicy antioxidant bass note from a pinch of cinnamon. Better yet, there's natural sweetness in the beets and berries, so there's no need to add a thing. If you choose frozen berries, you'll get an ice-cold frappé; with a little less apple juice, eat it with a spoon – or freeze for a couple of hours to make the perfect sorbet.

MIND, MEMORY & MOOD

DIGESTIVE HEALTH

HEART HEALTH

BLOOD-SUGAR BALANCE

BONE & JOINT HEALTH

HORMONE HARMONY

SKIN, SENSES & IMMUNITY

ENERGY BOOSTING

Beet the Blues Juice

SERVES 2

2 cooked beetroot, cut into chunks

150g fresh or frozen blackberries

100g fresh or frozen blueberries

300ml unsweetened apple juice or cold water

1/2 tsp ground cinnamon

Simply blitz all the ingredients in a blender until smooth, then pour into 2 glasses and serve.

Midlife Hack: No need to roast and peel fresh beetroot to get at the goodness. Buy ready-cooked (not in vinegar), grab from the fridge, rinse and go.

Health Tip
If you need cheering up, have a glass of beetroot juice; beets contain betaine, a compound that increases the production of serotonin, the body's natural mood-boosting hormone.

WHY WE LOVE IT

We know that we bang on about berries, but they really are a game-changer for anyone interested in midlife health – and cranberries are up there with the league champions for the impressive array of benefits they offer. The problem is that we rarely eat them raw; the cartons of cranberry juice we do consume tend to be over-processed, often containing as much sugar as cola. Our answer is this gorgeous Ruby Cooler, with the tart pop of frozen cranberries tempered by sweet watermelon, fresh mint and just a hint of honey.

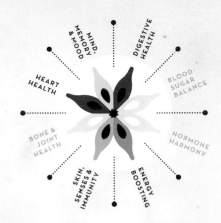

MIND, MEMORY & MOOD

DIGESTIVE HEALTH

HEART HEALTH

BLOOD- SUGAR BALANCE

BONE & JOINT HEALTH

HORMONE HARMONY

SKIN, SENSES & IMMUNITY

ENERGY BOOSTING

Ruby Cooler

SERVES 2

100g frozen cranberries

100g watermelon, peeled and deseeded

6 mint leaves

200ml cold water

1 tsp runny acacia honey

TO SERVE

ice cubes

about 300ml sparkling water

Put all the ingredients, except the ice and sparkling water, in a blender and blitz until smooth.

Pour into 2 glasses over ice, then top up with the sparkling water. Serve immediately.

Health Tip
Vit-rich cranberries boast a raft of benefits, from improving gut, brain and urinary tract health, to helping balance blood sugars and lowering the risk factors for heart disease.

WHY WE LOVE IT

Hibiscus tea is thought to have been the drink of choice of the Pharaohs; the clever old sticks might well have understood that hibiscus can provide an array of vitamins and help to lower blood pressure and cholesterol. Known as 'karkade' in Arabic, the steeped flowers of hibiscus (or rosella) produce a deliciously cooling and astringent drink, perfect for a sunny afternoon. Traditional methods require boiling, but cold steeping works equally well and retains more of the vital vitamins.

MIND, MEMORY & MOOD
DIGESTIVE HEALTH
HEART HEALTH
BLOOD-SUGAR BALANCE
BONE & JOINT HEALTH
HORMONE HARMONY
SKIN, SENSES & IMMUNITY
ENERGY BOOSTING

Karkade

HIBISCUS ICED TEA

SERVES 2

1 tbsp dried hibiscus flowers

500ml cold water

a squeeze of lemon or lime juice

2 tsp runny acacia honey

crushed ice, to serve

Combine all the ingredients in a bottle or jug, mix well and chill for at least 1 hour, or overnight.

To serve, strain the tea through a fine sieve or tea strainer into 2 glasses over crushed ice. The iced tea keeps well in the fridge for up to a week.

Try This...
Perhaps add these optional extras to your tea:
* 1 teaspoon grated fresh root ginger
* 2 teaspoons orange blossom or rose water
* A grinding of vanilla bean and a small handful of mint leaves
* Cloves and ground cinnamon

Health Tip
Hibiscus tea is ranked 'number one beverage' for antioxidant content (beating green tea), and it contains vitamin C – which probably explains its traditional use as a herbal remedy to fight off colds and infections by strengthening the immune system.

WHY WE LOVE IT

A green and grassy lemon tea, mellowed with a spoonful of honey – it sounds simple enough, but don't be fooled: matcha green tea is an impressive power powder, known to boost the metabolism, increase fat burning, help protect the brain and lower the risk of type 2 diabetes. Choose the best-quality matcha you can – it's expensive, but a little goes a very long way. Persevere with this one; it's an unconventional taste, but once you've got it, you'll never let it go.

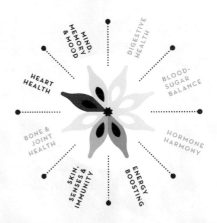

MIND, MEMORY & MOOD
DIGESTIVE HEALTH
HEART HEALTH
BLOOD-SUGAR BALANCE
BONE & JOINT HEALTH
HORMONE HARMONY
SKIN, SENSES & IMMUNITY
ENERGY BOOSTING

Chilled Matcha & Lemon Tea

SERVES 2

2 tbsp boiling water

1 tsp premium-grade matcha powder

500ml cold water

juice of 1/2 a lemon

1 tsp runny acacia honey

ice cubes, to serve (optional)

Pour the boiling water over the matcha powder and stir well to eliminate any lumps.

Stir in the cold water, lemon juice and honey, then chill until required.

To serve, stir the tea well, then pour into 2 glasses, over ice if you like.

Midlife Hack: This is lovely hot too – a great green booster for chilly days when the flu season is upon us.

Health Tip
Matcha contains potent polyphenols – notably EGCG, an antioxidant linked to low rates of heart disease. Studies have shown that women who regularly drink green tea had a 22 per cent lower risk of developing breast cancer, while men had a 48 per cent lower risk of prostate cancer.

WHY WE LOVE IT

This grown-up lemonade has just a little honey and a mellow backdrop of ginger and mint. It really hits the spot when you need hydrating but want something more exciting than water. Perfect for summer barbecues.

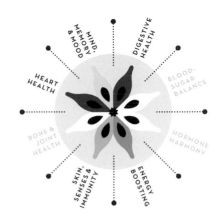

Ginger & Mint Muddle

SERVES 4

50g mint leaves, chopped, plus extra to serve

100g fresh root ginger, rinsed and thinly sliced (no need to peel)

2 tbsp runny acacia honey

juice of 2 lemons

1 litre boiling water

TO SERVE

ice cubes

slices of lemon

Place the mint, ginger, honey and lemon juice in a large heatproof jug and add the boiling water. Stir well and leave to steep for 30 minutes. Strain into a clean jug, then chill until ice cold.

Serve over ice with extra mint leaves and lemon slices. The lemonade will keep in the fridge for a few days.

Health Tip
Honey is known to have an inhibitory effect on 60 types of bacteria, giving it the reputation as one of nature's antibiotics.

WHY WE LOVE IT

This is one trendy drink at the moment – though switchel dates back to 19th-century American colonies, when it was apparently a favourite of thirsty farmers at harvest time. It has enjoyed a renaissance recently because we're beginning to acknowledge the health credentials of apple cider vinegar, particularly its benefits for insulin function. The thought of a vinegar drink may not immediately appeal, but it's all a matter of balance; adding honey, lemon and ginger – three more key Midlife ingredients – makes for an exceptionally delicious and refreshing drink.

MIND, MEMORY & MOOD
DIGESTIVE HEALTH
HEART HEALTH
BLOOD-SUGAR BALANCE
BONE & JOINT HEALTH
HORMONE HARMONY
SKIN, SENSES & IMMUNITY
ENERGY BOOSTING

Switchel

SERVES 2

500ml unsweetened cloudy apple juice or cold water

6cm piece of fresh root ginger, peeled and grated

2 tbsp apple cider vinegar

1 tbsp runny acacia honey

1 tbsp lemon juice

ice cubes, to serve

Heat all the ingredients in a saucepan and simmer gently for 2 minutes, stirring occasionally.

Strain the switchel through a fine sieve into 2 heatproof glasses or mugs and serve immediately. Alternatively, chill for an hour or more and serve over ice.

Midlife Hack: Try adding basil, lemon thyme or mint for a herby Switchel, or a cinnamon stick for a hint of spice.

Health Tip
Apple cider vinegar is a source of gut-friendly prebiotic plant compounds and has been shown to assist in blood-sugar control.

WHY WE LOVE IT

If you're a coffee addict (like us) then you'll know how great it is to have an alternative hot drink that you genuinely enjoy and, as in this case, is unbelievably good for you. This simple, aromatic infusion is a full-system reboot in a cup (if you inhale the steam it will give your head a good clear-out too). It makes a bright and refreshing morning brew, or a cleansing drink before bed.

MIND, MEMORY & MOOD
DIGESTIVE HEALTH
HEART HEALTH
BLOOD-SUGAR BALANCE
BONE & JOINT HEALTH
HORMONE HARMONY
SKIN, SENSES & IMMUNITY
ENERGY BOOSTING

Lemon, Ginger & Star Anise Tea

SERVES 1

5cm piece of fresh root ginger, rinsed and sliced (no need to peel)

2 slices of lemon

1 star anise

Place the ginger, lemon slices and star anise in a mug and add boiling water. Leave to steep for 5 minutes before drinking.

Health Tip
Our emblem in the Midlife Kitchen, the star anise has traditionally been used in Chinese medicine to support the immune system. More recently, scientific studies have confirmed that it contains four key compounds that have antibacterial properties.

WHY WE LOVE IT

A goodnight cuddle in a cup, this mellow chai is full of good things to soothe you to sleep. Almonds are a great evening ingredient as they contain tryptophan, an essential amino acid required to synthesise serotonin (the 'happy hormone') and melatonin (the 'sleep hormone'). The dash of date syrup gives a slight insulin boost to help tryptophan to cross the blood-brain barrier, while the almonds and nutmeg both provide magnesium to improve tryptophan conversion... But, hey, don't worry about any of that now. It's bedtime.

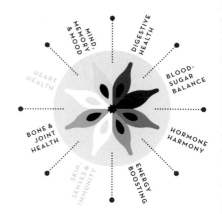

Bedtime Chai

SERVES 2

1 quantity Almond Milk (see right) or 500ml shop-bought unsweetened almond milk (see Midlife Hack)

4 cardamom pods, crushed

½ tsp ground cinnamon

a grating of nutmeg

a grind of vanilla bean, see page 211

1 tbsp Midlife Sweetener, see page 31, or date syrup

2 chai teabags

FOR THE ALMOND MILK

200g whole almonds, with skins on

600ml cold water, plus extra for soaking

sea salt flakes (optional)

To make the almond milk, soak the almonds overnight in water (this is important as it will produce a smoother, creamier milk, and it also activates enzymes which make the milk more nutritious).

The next day, drain and rinse the almonds. Put the nuts into a blender with the 600ml cold water and blitz for 3 minutes to form an opaque liquid. Strain through muslin, a jelly bag or a specialist 'nut-milk bag' into a clean jug, squeezing to extract as much almond milk as possible. Add a pinch of salt, if using. The milk will keep in the fridge for up to 2 days.

To make the chai, place 500ml of the almond milk in a small saucepan and bring to a simmer. Add the spices, vanilla and Midlife Sweetener or date syrup and simmer for a further minute or so. Remove the pan from the heat, add the chai teabags and leave to steep for 2–3 minutes.

Remove the teabags before serving, and use a milk frother if you fancy a frothy top.

Midlife Hack: Some commercial almond milks have a low almond content (as little as 2 per cent) and include added sugar, thickeners and emulsifiers such as carrageenan. If you do use shop-bought unsweetened almond milk, look for one with an almond content of 7 per cent plus.

Health Tip
A study published in the *Journal of Orthomolecular Medicine* found that when magnesium levels are too low, it's harder to stay asleep. Consuming magnesium-rich almonds and nutmeg (traditionally regarded as a cure for insomnia) should help you get good-quality sleep.

INDEX

AUTHORS' ACKNOWLEDGEMENTS

Producing *The Midlife Kitchen* has been the culmination of our long-held wish to work together – and it has been every bit as fun as we had hoped. Of course, creating a recipe book is a time-consuming affair, so our love and thanks go to our endlessly supportive husbands and kids: Paul, Lily and Ned (Mimi) and Rich, Rufus and Roxana (Sam).

We're lucky enough to have been surrounded by a uniquely talented team: our brilliant and wise agent Antony Topping at Greene & Heaton; our publisher Alison Starling, who shared our vision from the beginning and who led our dream team at Octopus – Jonathan Christie, Sybella Stephens, Caroline Brown, Matt Grindon and Saskia Sidey. We're incredibly proud of the photography on every page, so to our amazing shoot team – Issy Croker, Natalie Thomson, Linda Berlin, Stephanie McLeod and Nikky Richman – huge thanks for bringing our creations to life.

Thanks also to our consultant Dr Sarah Schenker, who made sure that everything we said was nutritionally sound.

Our original Midlife Kitchen star anise concept was brilliantly designed by Rachel Holtman at Surface Design www.surfacedesignconsultancy.com.

We'd also like to send a shout out to friends and places who have provided recipe thoughts and inspiration along the way: Nicola Williams, Michaela Van Nes, Debbie Spencer-Jones, Alex Hadfield, Avara Yaron, Chris Salans of the Mozaic Restaurant Group, the Yoga Barn Café, Café Batujimbar, Locavore and the many other great places we have eaten in Bali that sparked ideas for this book.

And finally, our special thanks to our inspirational mothers, Julie and Stephanie, because you can never show your mum enough gratitude (hear that, kids?).

An Hachette UK Company
www.hachette.co.uk

First published in Great Britain in 2017 by
Mitchell Beazley, a division of
Octopus Publishing Group Ltd
Carmelite House
50 Victoria Embankment
London EC4Y 0DZ
www.octopusbooks.co.uk

Text copyright © Mimi Spencer
& Sam Rice 2017
Design and layout copyright ©
Octopus Publishing Group 2017
Photography copyright © Issy Crocker 2017

ISBN 978 1 78472 318 7

A CIP catalogue record for this book is available from the British Library.

Printed and bound in Italy

10 9 8 7 6 5 4 3 2 1

Nutritional Consultant:
Dr Sarah Schenker

Publisher: Alison Starling
Managing Editor: Sybella Stephens
Copy Editor: Jo Murray
Creative Director: Jonathan Christie
Photographer: Issy Crocker
Photographer's Assistant:
Stephanie McLeod
Food Stylist: Natalie Thomson
Props Stylist: Linda Berlin
Senior Production Manager:
Katherine Hockley

MIMI SPENCER

Mimi Spencer is best known for co-authoring the 2012 best-selling book *The Fast Diet* with Dr Michael Mosley, which introduced the concept of 5:2 intermittent fasting to the world. *The Fast Diet* has sold more than a million copies worldwide, with translations into more than 30 languages, including Arabic, Hebrew and Taiwanese.

Mimi went on to write the subsequent recipe books *The Fast Diet Recipe Book* and *Fast Cook*. It was those books that developed her keen interest in nutrition and health, particularly concerning our changing requirements as the years go by – one of the main motivations for *The Midlife Kitchen*.

Her background is in lifestyle journalism, with an early career spent in London as a fashion writer for *Vogue*, the *Evening Standard* and then as editor of *ES Magazine*. She went on to become a columnist at *You Magazine (Mail on Sunday), Observer Food Monthly* and *Waitrose Kitchen*, while continuing to write lifestyle, fashion and food features for *The Times* and many national magazines.

Mimi, 49, lives in Brighton on the south coast of England, with her husband, two teenage children and an endlessly hungry dog.

SAM RICE

Sam Rice started out as a management consultant, but for the past 20 years has co-owned the travel business Ski Safari with her husband Richard. In 2013 she gained her WSET Diploma in wine and moved to Indonesia, subsequently writing about wine for *Inspired Bali* magazine.

Following the premature death of her youngest brother, who suffered from type 1 diabetes, she decided to overhaul her diet in the interests of living a longer and healthier life. She wrote about the process in her book *The Happy Eater, 4 Weeks to a Better Relationship with Food*.

Sam, 47, lives in the town of Sanur in Eastern Bali with her husband and two children. Eating for health is intrinsic to the Balinese way of life and this beautiful island has provided endless food inspiration as well as proving a fertile ground for recipe hunting.

Mimi and Sam met at the school gates and have remained firm friends ever since. They have always wanted to work together and *The Midlife Kitchen* is the perfect collaboration based on their mutual interest in fantastic, healthy food.

Dr Sarah Schenker, the book's nutritional consultant, is one of the UK's leading dietitians. She is further qualified as an accredited sports dietitian and registered public health nutritionist. Sarah has a wealth of experience as a health writer and broadcaster, regularly contributing to titles as diverse as the *Daily Mail*, *The Times*, *Men's Health*, *Cosmopolitan*, *Glamour* and *Top Santé* magazine, as well as appearing on and consulting for shows including *This Morning*, *Live with Gabby*, *Watchdog*, *Sky News* and across national and local BBC Radio. Sarah worked with Mimi Spencer previously on the international best-seller, *The Fast Diet Recipe Book*. She is also a member of the Association for Nutrition, The Nutrition Society, the Guild of Health Writers and has served on both professional and government committees.